MY T

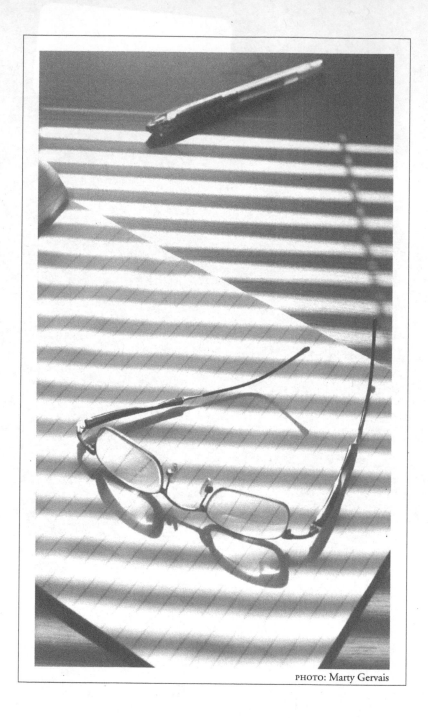

PHOTO: Marty Gervais

Faces of Windsor
MY TOWN

by
Marty Gervais

BIBLIOASIS

FIRST EDITION
Second printing, May 2016

Library and Archives Canada Cataloguing in Publication

Gervais, C. H. (Charles Henry), 1946–
My town / Marty Gervais.

Collection of newpaper columns published in *The Windsor Star*.
ISBN 1-897231-22-9

1. Windsor Region (Ont.). 2. Windsor Region (Ont.)—History. I. Title.
II. Title: Windsor Star.

FC3099.W56G47 2006   971.3'32   C2006-904688-3

COVER: Dan Janisse, *Windsor Star Photo*

*We acknowledge the support of the Canada Council
for the Arts for our publishing program.*

PRINTED AND BOUND IN CANADA

MIX
Paper from
responsible sources
FSC® C004071

ANCIENT FOREST ™
FRIENDLY

For Donna

Contents

Fighters, Rink Rats, Hockey Dads, Ballplayers . . .

Saints and Sinners

Nitwit Prophets, Dancing Novelists and a Barber's Son

Now, Let's Talk About Me

Foreword

WHEN MARTY GERVAIS LAUNCHED HIS "MY TOWN" COLUMN in the winter of 1997, he described one of his first subjects, Windsor author Harry Nielsen, as a writer who is "clear, crisp, witty, humorous at times . . ." Add another half dozen adjectives, including insightful, vividly descriptive and possessing a keen eye for detail, and Marty might have been painting a self portrait.

As the 10th anniversary of "My Town" approaches, Marty can rightfully say that he has introduced his readers to some of Windsor's most colourful characters. Perhaps of greater significance, Marty has drawn attention to dozens of other characters who might have otherwise flown under the radar, yet whose stories enlighten and inspire, forever connecting *The Star* to its community.

"My Town" has become a meeting place of sorts, with Marty's breezy style inviting one and all to join in the discourse. One can almost smell the coffee brewing and the muffins baking. When we handed him the gig nearly a decade ago, we asked Marty to bring personality to our pages. He has delivered in spades.

Perhaps owing to Marty's earlier incarnation as Religion Reporter for *The Windsor Star*, the editors often joke that his "My Town" characters typically fall under the category of saint or sinner—ex-hookers on one end of the spectrum and philanthropists on the other. Not too many fall in between.

In November 1998 we were looking for just the right reporter to tell the story of Windsor Spitfire forward Jeff Kugel—most certainly a sinner—who had been banned for life by the Ontario Hockey League following a wild melee at the Old Barn. As I scanned the newsroom for candidates, the thought occurred that Marty, with his deep affection for hockey, would be the ideal choice to bring Kugel to life.

He jumped at the chance. And what followed was a masterful account of a conflicted young man at the crossroads of adulthood. Marty wrote: "His six-foot-seven, 255-pound frame dwarfs his bedroom. Size 16 shoes—as large as twin skateboards—rest in front of the clothes closet. He slumps on the bed. Like Gulliver on the island of Lilliput. On the wall is a Wal-Mart framed photograph of a pair of worn skates. The aphorism below reads: 'It takes courage to have a dream and determination to make it come true.' Eighteen-year-old Jeff Kugel—banned for life by the Ontario Hockey League for an Oct. 25 altercation at Windsor Arena—ponders the reality of that dream. It's a dream many boys nurture when they start out—wobbly and awkward and naive on a pair of stiff skates in a cold arena—that some day they'll make it to the NHL."

"My Town" was conceived as a respite from the typically cold, cruel world of print journalism. We wanted more names, faces and souls in our paper. We wanted to feel connected to Windsor and Essex County, and to the countless Windsor ex-pats spread across Canada. We needed—and got—a storyteller.

As a columnist, author and University of Windsor English instructor, Marty has been a tireless promoter of the written word. Fittingly, he has agreed to allocate a portion of the proceeds from this book to Raise A Reader, the literacy program sponsored by *The Windsor Star* and its parent company, CanWest Global Communications.

In 25 years of journalism, I've met a lot of newsroom horn-tooters. But Marty Gervais isn't one of them. Soft-spoken and thoughtful, on the rare occasion he pitches his columns, it usually begins with, "I got a call from this guy." Which is exactly how the conversation began on a Friday in late March, when Marty came to tell me about a group of Presbyterians who were planning to occupy their church to prevent it from closure.

Marty not only broke the story of the Riverside Presbyterian Church sit-in, but also spent many nights at the side of the protesters, humanizing their doomed attempt to keep the place from being padlocked. They invited him back because they trusted him. They trusted him because he treated their plight with compassion. In the end they lost their battle, but went down swinging thanks to Marty's coverage.

In that particular instance, I suppose Marty was the saint. For *The Star* and its readers, his 10-year run has been a blessing.

—Marty Beneteau, *Windsor Star* Editor

RESTING ON THE FLOOR NEAR MY DESK is this bulky scrapbook of columns. I flip through it and realize this is how I have spent my life—pursuing stories, writing about people, tracking down individuals in coffee shops, arenas, on the street, at movie theatres. Also, it seems wherever I travel, someone is tapping me on the shoulder, and within minutes I am hearing a new story, new concerns, and who knows, maybe a whole new batch of lies.

In a way, I don't mind the half-truths. I have this insatiable desire to find out what people are doing. There's a word for that: busybody. My grandfather taught me years ago that the truth is only half the adventure—the other half is what you can make the listener imagine. As a journalist, I have a difficult time balancing it all out. I stick to the truth, but I have learned to dig a little harder, to find that moment in the lives of individuals that will enliven and make the story jump right off the page.

It seems I have always done that. As an example, I remember pestering my father one day about a man who lived at the end of the street. I was curious about him, and why he left the house every day at 10 A.M. and was back in half an hour, and then got in his truck and was gone for the rest of the day. I wanted to know what he did, where he went, why he wasn't married and why he lived in that big house. My father, telling me it was none of my business, reached into my schoolbag and pulled out the High Roads Dictionary that every student of my generation will remember. He read me the definition of a busybody: A meddlesome, prying, officious person.

"That's you!" he announced.

I felt bad.

Much later, I learned from Ecclesiastes, "God made man right and he hath entangled himself with an infinity of questions." Sure enough. Today I realize I've made that definition my business. I am a busybody with an infinity of questions. It's that curiosity about life that has kept me in search of stories. And this past year, that notion became abundantly clear. Like the time I found Don Gardiner, a goal judge in Sarnia. I had been to a hockey game to watch the Leamington Flyers play there. A boring game that got me pacing aimlessly in the arena. I saw this man stationed behind the Sarnia goal ready to flick on the light. I spotted the crutches nearby, and wondered what had happened to this man that he needed them.

That was my opening. It led to a story about this goal judge whose son was Mike Gardiner, a relief pitcher for the Detroit Tigers from 1993 to 1995.

Another tale that caught my attention was this fellow George Wiley, a Second World War pilot, whose name is among those at the Air Force Club. All these years, he was just a name on the list of those who died during the war. No one knew he had been among the seventy-six airmen who were immortalized in the film, *The Great Escape*. I discovered that it was Wiley's efforts to get his family in Windsor to send India ink, brushes and pens to him in the POW camp that led to the prisoners making the fake passports they were to carry with them to freedom.

I have written about arena life and where you can buy the best hotdog and popcorn; about the value of neighbourhoods and schools and the loyalties that grow up around them. There was also the story about an old trunk found at a garage sale in Amherstburg that contained correspondence about Henry Ford's secret plans to expand the company's manufacturing reach into Europe.

Each year has been interesting in its own way since I started writing this column in 1997. There's the story of Whitey Benoit, an old rumrunner who used to hawk hot diamonds for the Purple Gang in Detroit. I found him in a downtown apartment—now in his 90s—taking bets for the horses over the phone. He didn't mind if I used his name. He said, "Who's going to arrest a 90-year-old bookie?" True enough.

The stories I have found have been funny and sad. They have engendered anger and caused others to weep. They have moved people to action, with individuals sending money to my address in the hopes I would pass it on to the needy person I just wrote about. They have moved others to pause and write that I have made their day. They have caused others to correct me when I have been fed the wrong details.

I thank each and every one of these people.

I certainly don't remember all of the stories. But I have a feeling I will wake in the middle of the night in a nursing home at an advanced age—my mind a little scrambled—and my father will be standing there next me, shaking his head as he observes all these characters filing into the room. Believe it or not, I will remember each and every name. And I will bless each one for coming to see me.

Just watch.

Acknowledgements

The Windsor Star has given me great pleasure in writing this column for the news pages. The idea for it was born out of changes in the paper introduced by Gerry Nott and Marty Beneteau in 1997. They gave me the licence to seek out the "heroes" of our community. Permission to reprint these columns was given by *Windsor Star* publisher Jim Venney. I also have to thank a number of other individuals for the editing and proofreading of my work over the years. These include Tom McMahon, Harry Van Vugt, Gord Henderson, Karen Hall, Ted Shaw, Doug Williamson, Mike Frezell, Ellen van Wageningen and John Coleman. I must also acknowledge the assistance of Lindsey Rivait, Meighen Topolnicki and Melanie Santarossa on this project. And without the scrapbooks of these columns kept for me by Pam Bowsher, pulling this collection together would have been difficult. The library staff at the *Windsor Star*, including Denise Chuk and Ute Hertel were invaluable in their research. Special thanks must go to Marty Beneteau for his introduction to this volume and his faith in my work over the years. Publication of this work would not have been possible without the vision of Dan Wells and Biblioasis. Lastly, I want to thank all the people who came forward to tap me on the shoulder and offer their story, no matter how modest this account may have seemed in the grand scheme of things.

Battles, Escapes, Artificial Legs and Heroes

No Medals, No Ribbons

[Don Errey]

DON ERREY WAS A GERMAN PRISONER OF WAR when he bribed the guards with chocolate and cocoa so he could build an artificial limb for an airman who had lost his leg in battle. He constructed it from pieces of window frames, metal chairs, cotton batting, rubber from an old tire, leather from the soles of shoes, anything he could lay his hands on. He had scrounged for it all, swapping boxes of sweets with the guards for what he needed.

At first, it was just a curiosity. He was bored, rattled at spending his days during the war under the watchful eyes of the enemy. He was also a little tired of hearing this fellow soldier whining about having a leg amputated.

"I told him, 'C'mon stop your crying—I'll make you a leg.'"

"Of course I didn't know what I was doing."

Errey, who joined the Essex Scottish in Windsor in 1939 to go off to war, tells me this over the phone from London, Ont., where he now lives.

Over the years, from that moment at Dieppe when he glanced one last time at his brothers standing nearby on the beach, and bade them goodbye, he never realized he'd never see him again. Errey came to the aid of 349 others like his buddy. He rebuilt their limbs, fashioning special splints for crushed shoulders, broken ankles, and designed functional arms and legs.

In March 1944, when the Swedish exchange liner Gripsholm arrived in New York, 26 allied servicemen walked down the gangplank wearing what came to be called "the Errey leg."

Errey had become part of legend. Prisoners sought him out. Even his German captors encouraged him. When the war was over, he returned home to Wallaceburg. A hero. But he was never decorated. No medals, no ribbons, no humanitarian awards. Nothing. Just the memories. That was fine, because Errey didn't feel like sharing them. He turned everybody down. Even *Maclean's Magazine* and scores of newspapers. The way he saw it, the war was over. It was best to forget.

Deep down, however, it continued to gnaw at him.

"I didn't want to talk about it . . . I'd had enough—seeing these fellows with their legs blown off, no arms."

To this brash and sometimes gruff old soldier, those in the POW camps were the real heroes.

"It was pretty tough . . . I just wanted to forget."

His stepbrother Doug MacKenzie, only nine when Errey returned home in 1945, had heard the stories about what he'd done. And throughout his life, MacKenzie had wanted to write his biography. But Errey refused. The stories were locked up in his soul. He wouldn't open up.

Then 15 years ago, Errey acquiesced and began with his stories. MacKenzie burned up tape after tape of this quiet man detailing that moment at Dieppe, waiting on the beach, of his capture and life in a string of POW camps.

Finally, after all these years, Errey's gaining some recognition. His stepbrother, in collaboration with George Kerr, has written Errey's story, calling it *An Unlikely Hero: A Dieppe Survivor's Gift of Hope*.

Errey's proudest moment perhaps was three months after his liberation from Stalag 9C-Meiningen, Germany. That's when he stood on the mound at Briggs Stadium in Detroit right beside Bert Shephard, a pitcher with the old Washington Senators. Errey tossed out the traditional first ball of that three game series between the Tigers and Senators.

After the game, Errey and Shephard sat alone in the Senators' dressing room and reminisced about the war. How the two had met after the big leaguer had been shot down in an air raid over Berlin.

Shephard's only recollection of that battle was that just before losing consciousness, he looked down and saw "his blown off right leg hurtling earthward." Errey outfitted Shephard with an artificial limb. The air pilot was forever grateful.

Today, Errey, now 75, lives the irony of all ironies. He lies in a hospital bed, both legs having been amputated because of circulatory problems.

Maybe he's quietly down about it all, but he's never been one to cry in his beer.

"What's done is done," Errey says matter-of-factly. [Dec. 12, 1997]

Nazi Collaborator Couldn't Flee Her Past

[Sam Honig]

SAM HONIG DIDN'T TELL ME THE SIGNIFICANCE of our meeting Tuesday when he came downtown to show me some stories he had written for the Shaar Hashoymayim Synagogue's monthly newsletter. Stories from Poland. His past. Mostly from the war and what befell the Jews there.

Tuesday was the anniversary of the Nazi suppression of the 1943 revolt by the Jews in the Warsaw Ghetto. Sam, of course, knew the story. For his part, Sam survived the Nazis, fleeing Poland with his father and making his way to Russia. His story is contained in the autobiographical *From Poland to Russia and Back*, a book I helped him with.

I didn't realize, however, that he still had many other stories. And these have become popular reading at the synagogue. Some are terribly disturbing, like one about Stella, a former adolescent flame of his from Krakow who wound up becoming a Nazi collaborator.

Sam didn't learn of her activities until after the war. "That she became a Nazi mistress, most could forgive," Sam said. "Many would probably have done the same to save their lives, but Stella was also a collaborator and informer. Her life in the ghetto became luxurious, with the best clothing, furs and jewelry, the best food."

Stella never did any work and never wore the Star of David armband, as was required by every Jew. Nobody expected her to become an informer and coldly turn her friends over to the Gestapo.

Ironically, when she tried to save her parents from the camps, they refused. They were ashamed at her deeds. "In their eyes, they had lost their daughter," Sam said.

In 1946 when Sam returned to Poland and made inquiries about her, he was approached by two agents from the ministry of justice: "I got scared. I had no idea what they wanted. It was about Stella. They found out I was her school friend and had dated her . . . They heard how disappointed, angered and disillusioned I was over her criminal behaviour during the German occupation."

Sam was then asked to assist them in luring her back to Krakow to

21

face her accusers. But worried sick about carrying out this mission, he asked his father what he should do.

"We survived this terrible war," his father told him. "We lost most of our family and everything we possessed. I have only you. It isn't time to take unnecessary chances."

As it turned out, the agents tracked Stella to Hungary, but returned without her. They discovered she had become a mistress to "the highest ranking Russian officer in Hungary and lived in a well-guarded castle outside of Budapest."

After finishing school in Poland, Sam came to Canada and settled in Windsor. Occasionally, he'd think about Stella and wonder what had befallen her. It seemed that she'd vanished without a trace and "nobody heard or saw her."

Until one day, years later, in the U.S.

As Sam explained: "A friend of ours, a Krakow survivor, had an appointment with a gynecologist in a fashionable part of New York. When she entered the waiting room several ladies were seated and across from her was an extremely beautiful, elegant woman. Somehow she couldn't take her eyes off her. She felt that she had seen her before.

"After a while it occurred to her that the lady resembled Stella, yet the circumstances seemed so unlikely. But the more she looked at her with short glances . . . the more certain she was . . . She got up and approached her and greeted her by her first and second name.

"Stella got up, her face white, started to mumble some denials, grabbed her coat and ran out of the office.

"Instead of chasing after her, the woman managed to convince the receptionist to give her Stella's phone number. She traced Stella to a hotel and learned that she was married to a wealthy man and that they stayed in New York several weeks at a time."

That was the last time Sam heard of her.

"It is a sad story," Sam said.

"But who can explain or understand the unbelievable stress that people lived through during the Holocaust? I'm not sure what my reaction would be if I were to meet her after all those turbulent and trying years." [May 7, 2000]

Hand That Rocked The Cradle Won The War

[Maj. J.C. Tolmie, Florence Louck & J.R. Gay]

ONLY IN ESSEX. A year after the Great War. A year after the war against the German and Austrian empires that claimed 10 million lives, including some 60,000 Canadians.

Windsor did it in style. No mourning those deaths, as fellow columnist Gord Henderson reported in 1999. Instead, Windsor celebrated the anniversary of the armistice as a victory. There was a giant street party that included clowns, bands, animal acts, freak shows and a bare-knuckled riot. In other words, a downtown armistice carnival.

In Essex, it was a different matter. They waited until after Christmas. Indeed until Dec. 26th. A Friday night.

And what did the town of Essex do for its veterans? They held a debate to decide once and for all whether it was the civilians who won the Great War or the fearless soldiers slugging it out in the muddy fields of France.

The debate in the town hall was presided over by Maj. J.C. Tolmie, of Windsor. Yet it appears it wasn't all fierce debate, because they also trotted out to the delight of the town Miss Canada, Florence Louck, of Essex. She stood demurely on stage and waved to the delight of everyone, especially the young boys whistling at the back.

There was also a man in uniform sitting on a shell case who sang "Tenting Tonight," accompanied by the town's piano teacher. It reminds me of a comic scene out of Stephen Leacock's *Sunshine Sketches of A Little Town.*

Then the debate. Who really won the war? Those who stayed behind or those who went off to battle and risked their lives in a foreign land?

The mayor of Essex—then J.R. Gay—made an eloquent appeal to the court, citing the heroism, hardship and conquests of the soldiers who went overseas to fight the war to end all wars. He condemned those critics who would try "to rob them (these soldiers) of their glory." But under cross-examination, the mayor found himself stammering and admitting to the good work the people of his town had made towards the war effort.

23

Another witness was taken to task when he suggested if it weren't for the Canadian Army, this country might well be under the domination of communists. He cited the Winnipeg General Strike, rumoured as the start of another Bolshevik revolution. At that point, the lawyer for the people jumped to his feet, demanding, "Who stopped the formation of the soviets?"

The witness shot back: "The soldiers!"

The lawyer countered that the soldiers had returned home from the war, and were now civilians, so that argument wouldn't hold any water. The witness quibbled with this, pointing out, "But they were in uniform."

"So is the Salvation Army!" the lawyer responded.

The lawyer representing the army laid out a strong argument on the "profiteering" that went on at home, but this was dismissed when George Miller, lawyer for the people, waxed poetic. He told the court—as preposterous as it might sound—that nothing could compare to "the hardship of the poor farmer who had to rise an hour earlier every morning and then only got $3 a bushel for his wheat and $20 a hundred for his hogs," whereas the soldiers, "only occasionally were called out at such unreasonable hours."

Miller then cited how the mothers of these brave soldiers had "nursed" the army through its infancy, cared for it through its childhood, coached it through its boyhood and guided it into manhood. He claimed, "The entire credit (for winning the war) was due to the mothers of Canada's army."

The court closed, and spectators waited for the judgment.

Meanwhile, a Miss Finnie sang a wartime song to those crowded into the hall. The judges finally reappeared, looking stern and grave. Tolmie twisted his mustache and paused for a moment before finally speaking. It was clear to the judges: The real winners of the war were the moms.

So be it.

One can still see the town's piano teacher—a former president of the local Women's Christian temperance movement—sitting up proud and straight on her stool and looking ever so satisfied as her hands played yet another patriotic tune. [Nov. 26, 2001]

Neither Hero Nor Coward

[Stan Scislowski]

HE'S STANDING UP AND TELLING ME A STORY. He's got a make-believe Tommy gun cradled in his arms. He's weaving back and forth. Eyes flashing. He looks 20 again. The picture of youth. The short squat build of a rugged soldier. He's telling me about a raid he'd been on in Italy. Fighting the "Jerries," as he calls them even now.

Stan Scislowski, now 74, makes no excuses for what he did, or didn't do in the Second World War. That's what bothers him about the vets who cry in their beer because they didn't return heroes, or felt they could've shown more bravery. Stan sees them sitting in their silence and brooding, refusing to talk about the war. You did what you had to. Otherwise you died.

That's what Stan tells you in his memoirs, *Not All Of Us Were Brave*, a work that's taken 50 years to write.

Stan began the book in Italy. In the midst of battle. He'd turn to a scrunched up notebook, fold it back and write what he'd experienced. It was a way of "shutting" out the war, the noise, the carnage.

"I didn't smoke or anything—I'd sit there and nibble on biscuits and I'd write, trying to get my mind off things," he tells me in a voice raspy from throat cancer.

Like thousands of others, Stan had gone to war to become a hero. "I thought I'd come back and I'd be going up Ouellette Avenue in a ticker tape parade, and I'd be a national hero.

"Well, the first time I nearly got killed, I lowered my expectations from the Victoria Cross to maybe getting a medal for bravery . . . The second time, I thought maybe just being mentioned in some dispatches would be fine . . . Finally I was telling myself, 'Hell, I just wanna get outta here *alive!*'"

Stan returned from the war without a medal. That was fine. He came out alive. He had a future. Behind him were 18 turbulent months of battling on the front lines. Life as a soldier, as he calls it, sleeping in pup tents, marching through the night and bad weather, facing near death at every turn.

Stan wouldn't trade those years for anything. He returned home thanking his lucky stars he'd survived, and was ready to take on the world.

Stan was 19 when he joined the Perth Regiment in 1943. He's never forgotten the men who went overseas with him: "The good, the not-so-good, the funny and the sad, the beautiful, and the ugly, they are memories to treasure . . ."

Stan is a born storyteller. He spins yarns about using flamethrowers on the men in the latrines, just to scare them. He talks about getting lost behind enemy lines but meeting with some young fraulein, and letting the reality of war fade away. He laughs about the time he was wounded, and because of a threadbare denim tunic bereft of regiment patches, he was mistaken for a German officer, and couldn't get treatment from his own regiment.

Stan was even shot at by his own troops: "I yelled, 'What the hell are you shooting at? I'm a Canadian . . . I live at 1720 Parent Avenue, Windsor, Ontario!'"

Moments of levity kept him sane. Attending a British musical at an Italian Opera house, he sat in a box seat right next to the stage, and could look up at the tiers where "the officers sat with their lady escorts—prostitutes in other words . . .

"And during the intermission, I saw something floating down from the upper tiers . . . Looked like a balloon.

"It turned out to be a condom someone had blown up, and it bounced about with everybody hitting it.

"Then it suddenly burst and there was absolute silence for about a minute, then I could see all the guys reaching into their tunics and pulling out condoms and blowing them up . . .

"There must've been 500 of them floating about in the opera house."

Stan wrote the story years ago, but the Legion Magazine turned it down on moral grounds.

Stan doesn't boast about his exploits. He tells you straight: "I was no hero type, neither was I a coward . . . I was just one of hundreds of thousands . . . somewhere between the two extremes. I did my job."
[July 10, 1998]

Battle Of River Canard

[Lyle James]

HERE'S A MAN WITH THE DISTINGUISHED FLYING CROSS from the Second World War. Here's a man whose plane was shot up over Germany flying some 32 missions, but neither he nor his flight crew ever once got hurt.

At least not in Germany.

The battle over River Canard was another matter.

Some of the old families around there know all about that stormy grey day in November 1942 when Lyle James darted overhead in a Tiger Moth. He was just finishing his training before being shipped off to England. The way James explains it, "the devil squeezed into our cockpit," and suggested "a little unauthorized low flying."

James and his instructor, Sgt. Al Beaudoin, decided to indulge in a little fun chasing some ducks out of the water.

As James swooped over these birds on River Canard, they didn't budge. He must've been only 10 feet above the water, then realized "they were the most realistic decoys he had ever seen.

"They just sat there perfectly docile and contented!"

But James also felt "a thud" at the tail wheel.

"So we decided to go back and see if we'd hit something."

The instructor figured the engine probably misfired. But as they circled back, James spotted three duck hunters standing up in the collapsed duck blind that had just been sheared off at the roof.

"I guess we'd tore the roof right off. And you can imagine those three duck hunters in there, half frozen, sharing a bottle of wine, and all of a sudden this plane rips the top off . . .

"Anyway, these three hunters were standing up, aiming right at us . . . Before I could say 'Jack Robinson,' I saw flames come from the barrel of each gun . . ."

James couldn't avoid it. You would've thought he was looping away from an avenging Messerschmitt. Too late. The shotguns let loose, scattering 200 pellets into the canvas-like exterior of the plane, peppering his arms, legs, and butt. It felt like "red hot needles." James hightailed it, climbing away from the scene, sore from the blasts, and worried sick over what he'd tell the CO.

"With one volley, those duck hunters had won the battle over River Canard," chortles 80-year-old James from his home in Sarnia.

His instructor had blood running down his face from where he'd been hit over the eye. The two faced court martial if the truth was known—intentionally damaging one of "His Majesty's aircraft."

But how could they explain being fired at? Over Canada? This wasn't Germany! There was no war here.

When they returned, James had already concocted the tale. How they'd been flying over Lake Erie, near Leamington, and had come out of the clouds, when suddenly they were hit. The two pilots never expected so much attention from the story.

"You can't imagine the fuss—two aircrew wounded and 200 holes in the plane!"

Police and reporters swarmed the two when word got out. Worse was the decision of the Mounties to track down those hunters. James had to go back up in a plane to show exactly where they'd been hit.

As they coasted over Leamington ("I had never been there before in my life") James peered below at the lakeshore and the beautiful residential homes.

"A mouse would've been out of place there . . . Then I spotted a ravine and told them that's where the shots had come from.

"As it turned out, when the Mounties went to investigate, they found two shotgun shells . . . case closed!"

James went off to war. And of the 15 RCAF crews with whom he had gone over to England, his was the only one that finished its tour of operation.

"I brought aircraft back from Germany all shot to hell and I was chased and shot at by (German) deadly night fighters, but never once got a single piece of flak in me. You know, we were the only two airmen ever to be wounded in an aircraft in Canadian air space . . ."

Since the war, James has tried to search out those three hunters. He knows that two of them have since passed away. The one still alive—about the same age—hasn't come forward.

James doesn't know his name, but would love to meet the man and buy him a drink. [Oct. 3, 1997]

The Bombing Of Comber

[Bruce Fox & George Danckaert]

BRUCE FOX HAD BEEN OUT SHOOTING SQUIRRELS AND RABBITS, without a care in the world until the police rolled up and started firing questions at him. He was a scared kid, barely 15, worried sick, probably stammering a little while explaining his whereabouts that grey fall day in November 1942. The police were searching for the hunters who had shot up a Tiger Moth plane used by two airmen in a training session. The story behind this bizarre shooting incident is known as The Battle of River Canard. People around that area still speak about it. A story passed down from one generation to the next. How two airmen—weeks away from going off to fight in the Second World War—were having a little fun swooping down over River Canard and scaring some ducks. They accidentally sheared off the top of a duck blind and when they looped back for a second look, three outraged hunters stood like defiant soldiers, raised their rifles and blasted some 200 holes of buckshot into the plane. Fearing court martial, the pilots lied and told their C.O. and the police how they'd been hit somewhere in the Leamington area. Later when asked to be more specific, they pointed out a small ravine closer to Kingsville.

The spot the airmen had pointed out was one of Fox's favorites. That's where they found him. Right off the Graham Side Road. Standing there with a .22 rifle at his side. Like a murderer with a smoking gun. "I was about two miles out of Kingsville, right there in that gully when the cops picked me up." Fox was questioned for more than an hour about the incident but was released because the police were searching for someone with a shotgun, and all he owned was a .22. "The police scared me right to death," says Fox. After reading my column, the former transport driver, now 70, telephoned a friend and told him: "After 55 years, I guess I'm finally exonerated . . ."

All these years he'd wondered about that incident, and what really happened. All that he'd been told was that someone had fired at a plane over that gully. He knew nothing about River Canard. The friend Fox called was another retired trucker, 68-year-old George Danckaert, who has his own share of stories about "those flyboys" (as

29

he calls them) whose initial air training was done out of the Windsor Airport. He called them "crazy." They terrorized the county farmers with their antics.

Danckaert will tell you these flyboys may have lost The Battle of River Canard, but their mates won the Battle of Comber. He was only about 13 at the time, when some exuberant airmen in training touched down in a field near Comber, and loaded up with tomatoes. The planes then roared low over the town and did a kind of a barrel roll and let the tomatoes tumble out over the sleepy farm community. "They bombed Comber!," says Danckaert who laughs about the incident now. "I was just a kid then," says Danckaert who grew up in the Ruscom area, "and they'd come flying over, and come down so low they'd barely miss you, and you'd hit the dirt—they'd scare the devil right out of you." Other times, these flyboys would angle and squeeze dangerously in between the H. J. Heinz chimneys in Leamington. "And they'd clip telephone lines . . . They catch the lines and they'd have about a hundred feet of telephone wire wrapped around their wings." Danckaert remembers pickup trucks passing by the farm with Tiger Moth wings stacked in the back from crashes.

When Danckaert and Fox now get together they jaw about the good old days, and laugh at those years when pilots, anxious for the taste of war, treated Essex County like the Battle of the Bulge. As for Fox, he can finally put to rest the mystery about what happened that day in November 1942. If he'd had a shotgun with him when the police nabbed him, he might have had a hard time claiming that his only targets were squirrels. [Oct. 16, 1997]

Windsor's Great Escapist

[Flight Lt. George William Wiley]

HE WAS ONE OF THEM. This fellow from Windsor. Twenty-three years old when he was machine-gunned down by the Gestapo. He had made a run for freedom. He was one of the 76 that had been locked behind barbed wire in a German concentration camp. One of the 76 who tunnelled his way to freedom. One of the 76 who helped to sink shafts, build underground railroads, forge passports and maps, fashion fake weapons and tailor German uniforms, all with the intention of running for freedom.

Running for home.

Flight Lt. George William Wiley of Windsor, in the dark March night in 1944, escaped from this Nazi stalag that held some 10,000 prisoners of war. Found himself sliding in the darkened tunnel, gravel toppling over him, and then shimmying up through a hole like a rabbit and running for the woods. His heart pounding. His legs like lightning as he darted into the night.

An escape that would later be immortalized in the 1963 Academy Award winning film called *The Great Escape*.

This week I went in search of George W. Wiley to find out who he was. I wound up talking to those who had been in that camp with him. And though they don't remember him specifically, they told me what it was like at Stalag Luft III in March 1944 when 76 airmen made a mass escape through underground tunnels.

For Wiley, it meant death. He was rounded up with six other airmen and shot by Gestapo Chief Wilhelm Scharpwinkel and his flunky associate Hans Lux. The next day, they executed 10 others. And days later, nine more.

Among those executed by the Gestapo were six Canadians.

Of the 76 who ran for freedom, 50 were tracked down and killed on a directly-signed order from Hitler himself, who was incensed at this embarrassing incident. His order resulted in 70,000 uniformed Germans hunting down the 76 escapees.

But who was George Wiley?

To the RAF, he was Serial No. J7234. Flew with the 112 Squadron, named Swift in Destruction. His Kittyhawk aircraft was shot down March 10, 1943, some 45 miles northwest of Tatauin, Egypt. That day, his squadron lost six pilots to the Nazis. He was taken prisoner, shipped to Europe and incarcerated at Stalag Luft III.

A year before his capture in October 1942, Wiley had been in a battle over the desert and had to make a "wheels up" landing with his damaged Kittyhawk near El Daba, Egypt. But he managed to escape capture.

But who was he? Who were his parents? Did he have a girlfriend? Who remembers him?

Well, the Air Force Club of Windsor, which lists Wiley's name among the dead, would like to know. They want information on whether he still has family here. According to Bernie Riendeau, a trustee of the club, they were unaware until now of Wiley's connection to the Great Escape. He says it's not likely Wiley did his training here. My search brought me to Omer Levesque of Aylmer, Quebec. This curmudgeonly old pilot, now 80, is sure he knew him from the camp, but only remembers the name now.

"That's because my buddies were all with the RCAF (401 "Westmount" Squadron), and he was with the RAF (as were 60 per cent of Canadian airmen) . . ."

Levesque bunked with the legendary Wally Floody, the tunnel king, whose character in the film was played by Charles Bronson. He died twelve years ago.

"He was a hard rock miner from Kirkland Lake . . . Six-foot four," recalls his widow Elizabeth Floody, who said her husband dug these tunnels 30 feet deep. "He nearly died in them when they collapsed on him, and twice he was buried alive."

Floody and Levesque never made the escape—they were transferred to a camp 10 miles away two weeks earlier.

Levesque has a thousand stories, and begins them in this way: "I wasn't shot down . . . I was having the best day of my life over the North Atlantic—I had shot down three 190s when the Rolls Royce engine in my Spitfire overheated, just like in a car, and I went down . . . I was scooped up by the Germans like a fish out of the water . . .

"The next thing I knew I was sitting at the Captain's table with bandages around my head and listening to Beethoven's 5th . . . I knew I wasn't in England!"

Levesque was a tunneller like Floody. A mole in the sand.

"I don't know how things would've turned out had I escaped," he mused.

As for Wiley?

There's some confusion as to when he was actually killed. Some records indicate it was the same night he escaped, March 25, 1944. But the Public Records Office in London England shows it was March 31.

Wiley was part of that group of airmen who made the 18,000 sorties to remove the sand in the small makeshift "sausage" bags, dispersing it around the compound.

He was among those who snatched up 4,000 bed boards for the tunnel shafting, 1,699 blankets, 34 chairs 52 20-man tables, 478 spoons, 30 shovels, 1,000 feet of electrical wire, 600 feet of rope, 76 benches, 246 water cans, and 582 forks.

All in aid of freedom.

"Wiley was part of it—everyone was. We wanted out!" says Levesque. [Feb. 19, 2001]

Carhops, Smugglers, Diners, Ice Cream Parlours

"The Ghost Of Abars" And Other Stories

[Freddy Peltier]

IF YOU GET A CHANCE, STOP BY THE PLACE, have a last drink, bid good-bye to one of the great watering holes in Windsor.

Its future is uncertain.

Last week, bar owner Paul Susko saved Abars from the wrecking ball. At least for a few more months. Hopefully longer. At the moment, Susko doesn't know who has bought this ramshackle old building, and doesn't even know to whom he will pay the rent. His intention however is to lease the bar as long as he can. But up until a couple of days ago, Susko had expected he'd have to shut the doors at the end of this month.

And that would have been it for Abars, this old roadhouse bar that hugs the Detroit River in old Riverside, sitting at the foot of Lauzon. It's a place that reeks with beer and sweat and history. A place that has spawned a host of "characters," including the legendary Freddy Peltier, the barrel-chested man with a ferocious temper who patrolled the nearby Peche Island with a 12-gauge shotgun. The river was his main street, and Abars his hangout, the place where this 240-pound river rat held court. He'd stand at one end of the bar, have a smoke, drink by himself, and chat up Walter Dutka, its former owner, who called Peltier "the meanest SOB" he'd ever met.

But there were other characters. Indeed, a legion of men and women who gave this old bar a colourful and lively history. At one point, the place was designated as the *Windsor Star*'s "Eastern Bureau," because so many of the newsroom's boys gathered here.

Its earliest link to history however is to the high rolling Prohibition period when this was a roadhouse run by the eccentric, jewelry-laden Mrs. Hebert (hence the anglicized name "Abars"). Her establishment attracted the likes of Al Capone, the Purple Gang and others. The Dutka family took over Abars in 1951, and owned it up until a few years ago. In those days, beer sold for 10 cents a glass. As Walter Dutka will tell you, "For a buck, you could get corned!"

This former bar owner, who took over the place from his parents, has a million stories to tell. Like the one about the man who leaned over the bar one night, and told Walter how not even his dog loved him.

"I am going to go and jump in the river!" he said. And he did just that. Actually cut a hole in the ice and slipped into the icy depths below.

Another time, a fellow ambled in and ordered a double Tom Collins.

"I knew he didn't drink," said Walter, "so I asked him, 'What's up?' And he says, 'I'm going home to shoot my wife.'

"About a half hour later, the cops came in . . . This guy had actually gone home and shot his wife with a .22 rifle."

Then there's the ghost of Abars. Upstairs. Walter's parents believed it existed, and blamed it for changing the clocks in the middle of the night, or turning the lights off and on, or shifting the plants around, or toppling over furniture.

"He also used to dance up there on the linoleum, soft shoe stuff," claims Walter.

Abars is among the last of the old roadhouses. Gone already are both Thomas's Inn and the Rendezvous. About the only place still operating from that era is Danny's, a male strip establishment on Riverside Drive.

And so the story goes, the tale behind Danny's—once known as the Belle-Vue—is that during the Roaring Twenties it was lost on a roll of the dice.

If Abars is bulldozed to make way for residential development, it'll be yet another part of this area's history vanishing. More than that, it'll be missed.

When Walter sold the bar in 1997, he knew he'd miss it, and told me, "I sure loved those people. We were one big family." For him, walking out of Abars nearly four years ago was one of "the saddest days" of his life. It was in this neighbourhood bar where Walter grew up, sweeping floors and washing dishes, that he heard so much of the private moments of joy and turmoil of people, so much about their families and friends.

Walter was a good listener, heard it all. Saw it all.

Go have a drink. Be a part of history. [Jan. 22, 2001]

How To Be A Canadian

[Dan Beaudoin]

YOU CAN'T MISS IT. This modest house at the corner of Lincoln and Erie is red and white. It is adorned with Canadian flags. The front gate bears a painting of the Canadian flag. Embedded in the sidewalk leading to the front steps is a metal maple leaf. The railings of the porch are trimmed in red. The front door is red. Inside, it's more of the same.

Red doorframes.

A red kitchen table.

Red chairs.

A red ceiling fan.

Red-trimmed bathroom mirrors.

Red medicine chest.

Red stairway.

Red floors.

Red electrical outlets.

Dan Beaudoin sits across from me. He's sipping from a coffee mug decorated with maple leaves. He's wearing an "I am Canadian" shirt, and a red maple leaf pin.

As my eyes scan this small, two-bedroom home, I see still more. Over Dan's bed there's a Canadian flag. On one wall, he has painted a mural of the flag, floor to ceiling in size, the full wall. There's a red neon sign with a Canadian flag in the side window. I can see his red Dodge Ram parked in the driveway. A miniature Christmas tree is tucked away on a shelf. It is decked out in red and white trim with a red Santa hat perched atop its branches.

A peek inside the bathroom reveals a red shower curtain, even a red toothbrush.

This guy's nuts, I think.

To that, Dan Beaudoin merely shrugs: "Oh well . . . That's the price you pay for patriotism."

That's what it's all about for this 49-year-old Canadian Salt Company worker. He doesn't care what people think of his obsession. He sees it grounded in this love of country. Most pay little attention to the fact he may have gone overboard. His kids don't mind. His ex-wife doesn't mind. His fellow Salt workers don't mind. And for the newcomers to his house, Dan rewards them with a pen emblazoned with a Canadian flag and a notebook with the word CANADA on it.

He hands this to me: "This is for you—I give this to everyone who comes here for the first time. You can write your story of Canada in it."

His patriotism is simple. It's not an outgrowth of a vast reading of Canadian history. He probably couldn't spiel off the names of Canada's prime ministers. Or tell you how many Canadians died in the great wars. Or recite the words to Robert Service's "The Cremation of Sam McGee."

Then again, most other Canadians can't either.

Maybe that's the point.

Patriotism is in the heart. This beating pride for his country, for its traditions. Why try to understand or explain it? It simply means embracing everything about your country. And Beaudoin does that. Even wearing a Montreal Canadiens jacket. Or propping up a hockey trading card of Maurice "The Rocket" Richard on the television.

Or driving his red truck through city streets with flag waving on Canada Day.

"I love this country, and everything there is about being Canadian."

On July 1, Beaudoin bought a slab of cake decorated with a Canadian flag and cut it up for his friends at his favourite bar. He then handed out miniature Canadian flags, and with his buddies toasted his country.

"It's just this overwhelming love for this country. I can't explain it."

The house on Lincoln is so obviously steeped in Canadiana that it drew the attention of an immigrant couple who knocked on its door.

Dan opened the door to an elderly couple standing on the porch.

"Can I help you?" he asked.

And the lady inquired: "Yes, is this the immigration place?"

One would think that.

Question the kids in the neighbourhood, and they'll tell you. Everybody calls Dan Beaudoin's place, "Canada House." [July 14, 2000]

Dairy Freez

[Click Wright]

IT'S LIKE OPENING DAY BASEBALL. You look forward to it and hope the weather will hold. You roll the dial on your radio to locate the "Oldies" station, tune into Ray Charles singing "Hit The Road Jack!" or Pat Boone crooning "April Love." You coast into the parking lot, flash your lights and watch the carhops saunter over to the car. This could be 1958 or 1964.

You could be wearing a ducktail haircut. You could be thrumming the dashboard like a keyboard to the cranked-up music booming from the radio.

You could be James Dean. You could be . . .

But this is 2005, not the 1950s, and you can't carry a tune. You don't even remember most of the lyrics to the Oldies, but the music still throbs in your veins all the same. And this is not California. This is old Highway 3 in North Ridge between Essex and Cottam. This is the Dairy Freez.

A throwback to another time.

A place that's been operating for 51 years.

A place where the owner's grandfather predicted his son would lose his shirt if he dared open this ice cream stand.

Three generations later, the place thrives on the sale of ice cream, hamburgers and footlong hot dogs. Each March—usually the end of March—the place reopens.

"But we don't tell anybody about it. We don't announce it," says owner Mike Reaume. "We just open up, and then work out the bugs, making sure everything is operating.

"But we usually get someone stopping by and saying it's a sign of spring and that when we open it means the winter is over."

This past weekend—three glorious days of sunshine—was proof that old man winter has finally been booted out. Business was so brisk, it was like the height of summer in a place that sells more than 30,000 24-ounce milkshakes a season.

Rituals surround this highway carhop. They begin with a ride out to the country. Everyone with the same idea.

41

On Sunday, I pulled into the place to find a sea of automobiles zig-zagged in the parking lot, windows rolled down and the music pumping out like there was no tomorrow. I could see the burgers and fries and the mile-high cones and footlongs being passed through the car windows.

Life on a Sunday afternoon.

A footlong with onions and mustard and a thick ice-cold chocolate shake—done in the old fashioned way in a replacement blender that cost Mike another $900 this year.

Nothing like it. And a ballgame on the radio.

Dairy Freez has been in the same family's hands for five decades. It was started by Click Wright when he swiped the idea from a place in Ingersoll in the 1950s. When he got back to North Ridge, he set up the business.

Four decades ago, he installed the sign that sits out front even to this day. A family business. One where his own kids and grandkids, all of whom worked Friday and Saturday nights till one a.m., toiled all summer as carhops or cooks.

In 1998, the place was sold to Click's daughter, Arlene, who spent all of her summers here. She and her husband, Mike, however, have put their own stamp on it, every year introducing something different.

"We're trying turkey burgers this year," Mike says. "We tried them out during the winter, and we thought, 'Well, this is different, why not?'"

Time will tell.

Meanwhile the outlet goes through more than 1,000 burgers a weekend, and hundreds of hot dogs.

There's a sense of history to the place. Maybe not history with a capital "H." But it's history just the same. The Dairy Freez is a fixture in the lives of Essex County residents. A place where men have made proposals to girlfriends. Even weddings have been celebrated here.

A few years ago, I heard a story about how a crop duster landed his plane in the open field back of the ice cream place, dusted himself off and ambled across the field. He assured everyone he wasn't having engine problems.

He simply wanted an ice cream cone. [April 12, 2005]

Memories Of A "Sacred Spot"

[Glengarda]

THE SUN STREAMS THROUGH THE WINDOWS, making patterns on the smooth hardwood floors and the empty walls. Down the hall, the chapel, shorn of its icons, except for one large wooden cross, leaded windows, and empty choir stalls, speaks of a silence and a presence from a past that soon will disappear.

Even so, those days are not forgotten by the Ursulines who used to inhabit this space, rising at 5:30 A.M. for prayers. They still live with the joy of those treasured moments, of days filled with prayer and work.

And last summer, when the handful of sisters remaining at Glengarda decided to vacate and sell the place, they were joined by others of the order—some in wheelchairs—who had lived here over the years. They went room to room, on a pilgrimage of their own history, their roots in this community, the lives they had lived together.

"We went through the whole house and told stories of people we remembered," says Sister Theresa Mahoney, a member of the Ursuline's leadership committee that opted to sell the building and the three-hectare site on Riverside Drive East.

That moment last July was celebrated without fanfare, solely by strolling the halls of this rambling building put up in 1939.

"We talked about the memories, the families who came to visit, the children being baptized, the mopping up of floods in the basement. We can't forget the blood and sweat and tears that went into this place."

Yet that tour wasn't an odyssey into regret or sentimentality. It involved no sadness over the passing of an era. Rather it was a quiet, joyful ritual, a comforting blend of humour and buoyant sentiment.

"It was our way of dealing with this decision," says Sister Theresa. She insists on selling the property to developer Chuck Mady, who plans to demolish the 58-year-old former convent and school, the sisters weren't turning their backs on the memories, or Windsor itself.

"Glengarda's a sacred spot, a holy spot, and we won't forget it, but it's time for us to move on."

The Ursulines, explains Sister Theresa, face the future differently. It's not a matter of wiping away the past. The sisters can't lament that Glengarda—rich with its own history and stories and accomplishments as a school—will be demolished.

"We have to sell without any strings attached."

But in selling, Sister Theresa adds, "We're not abandoning Windsor . . . We just didn't say 'the heck with this.' It's simply this building is no longer helpful to us in ministering to people."

As Sister Theresa makes her way through the darkened hallways of the former convent, passing empty rooms that at one time had so much vitality, she says, "I don't know if other people assume we don't care . . . We do care."

But this former principal believes the role of the Ursulines in Windsor has changed dramatically since 1919, when the order acquired the McGregor farm that extended in a 28-hectare strip of land from the Detroit River to Tecumseh Road. Over the years, the nuns disposed of much of the property, including parcels to Brennan High School and Our Lady of Guadalupe Church. The present building with its stately bell tower was the result of Sister Kathleen Taylor's efforts when she arrived here in the 1920s. She had envisioned a sprawling school to accommodate the trainable mentally challenged.

Over the years, that mandate was modified numerous times. Today, Glengarda Child and Family Services, now a provincially sponsored agency (no longer under the jurisdiction of the Ursulines) counsels and provides education to some 66 emotionally troubled children.

The group still occupies Glengarda, and plans to move out in the next few months. In its heyday, Glengarda dispatched sisters to teach in Catholic schools throughout the area. It also boasted a music academy. All of that gradually changed.

"That's the way it should be. We're here to serve. We go where we're needed," says Sister Theresa.

A maxim perfectly in keeping with the Ursuline founder, the 16th-century Saint Angela Merici, who had ruled how essential it was "to read the sign of the times and adapt."

Today, Ursulines work among street people, refugees and support groups for women.

"People may not see us in schools or hospitals, but it doesn't mean we've gone away."

The move out of Glengarda was partly necessitated by finances. Like other religious orders, the Ursulines face a crisis of dwindling numbers and an aging membership.

At one time the order had more than 600 members. Now, there is less than half that number. And the 40-bed infirmary at the motherhouse in Chatham is overflowing.

In days past, that would have been fine, when the Ursulines provided their own nursing staff. Now the order must resort to hiring nurses.

"We used to do everything ourselves . . . We cooked, cleaned . . . We were administrators, childcare workers, teachers . . . We no longer have the kind of energy to go day and night."

Standing at a tiny window in a cubbyhole room on the third floor, Sister Theresa says, "This is where I stayed when I lived here. The river was the first thing I saw in the morning, and the last thing I saw at night."

A good memory. Yet there's an air of expectancy about what lies ahead for her and for others in her order.

"We are on the brink of seeing a whole new form of religious life . . . We have a pretty good sense of adventure and realism about the future." [Mar. 26, 1997]

Hudson's Shoppers Elevated Smuggling To An Art

[J. L. Hudson's Department Store]

THERE WAS A WOMAN WHO USED TO HOP ON A TUNNEL BUS to Detroit wearing only a raincoat, a pair of underwear and a bra. A few hours later she'd be back on the bus returning to Windsor, decked out in chic J. L. Hudson's department store purchases.

That story of smuggling is a stitch in the fabric of Windsor's past, of what it was like living on the border through the 1940s and '50s, and one of the things people remembered when they heard Thursday how this hulking dowager towering over Detroit's Woodward Avenue finally was going to come toppling down.

Few, if any, may have given this 25-storey building any thought in recent years. It has stood like a pyramid—terribly silent, sad and forgotten amid the festering wounds of a city ravaged by riots and neglect. But for some on the south side of the Detroit River who remember its glory years—right down to the multitude of elevators with those kindly attendants, the spectacular mezzanines of garments and jewelry, the Christmas décor—the news Thursday was like learning of an old friend passing away.

It was a sign of how little reverence may be left in our souls, when we can't save something of our past.

That was the feeling of 95-year-old Camilla Stodgell Wigle, who helped save the former Barclay building of the Hiram Walker complex on Riverside Drive. She called the proposed demolition of Hudson's—once the grandest and largest department store in the world—more than "a shame."

"Why is it that they want to tear this down? Why do they want to tear down everything that's old?"

For her, Hudson's was a tangible symbol to Detroiters of what could be. It seemed to hold out hope. And because of that, there was always something far more alive in its presence than the $500-million Renaissance Center.

"With Hudson's, there's a veritable living past that breathes stories and memories. I don't like seeing things destroyed," Wigle said.

It's a view that might not be shared with developers and politicians across the river, but on this side, Leila Pepper, a writer and long-time friend of Wigle's, feels its disappearance strikes at the heart.

"There isn't anyone who doesn't know about Hudson's in Windsor," she said. "We all had a part in it."

Pepper's youth lies within its history. She has vivid memories of those adolescent arrangements made with friends to rendezvous on the first floor, "just inside that first entrance" at the cosmetic counter.

"Or we might go upstairs to the restaurant and have lunch.

"That's when you could walk around downtown and not be afraid."

Of course, smuggling was as much a part of the routine of city people as going to Sunday mass. And that's why you didn't see much of those trademark green boxes of Hudson's goods coming back here.

"I didn't smuggle," maintains Pepper, "because my father was the manager of the Salt Company, and he thought we should spend our money here in Windsor.

"But a million of my friends shopped over there, and they took it back to Windsor."

Pepper is the one who told me the story of the friend in a raincoat: "She'd just go over wearing nothing but underpants and a bra, and never got caught. She'd come back (to Windsor) wearing slips, a dress, anything."

Wigle still laughs at another friend who snuck past Canada Customs with drapes wrapped tightly around her waist "all tucked up with pins. . . . But one of the pins must've fallen out because part of the drapes had come down and was hanging below her coat.

"The customs officer said to her. 'My goodness, you're losing your petticoat.'"

Back in the 1950s on Saturday nights, on those days just before school started in September, if you drove around Hudson's, you'd see queues of cars with Canadian license plates. You'd see fathers standing on the sidewalk, dutifully reaching in through the open windows of their cars and taking weathered-white jeans, shirts and shoes and tossing them into the wire trash cans.

And if you looked closely, you'd see the elbows and legs of kids contorting inside as they yanked on yet another pair of jeans to smuggle back.

I remember such scenes. There was the day my father drove back from Hudson's with five boys crammed into his Plymouth. All of us sweating and gasping for air. And I remember when my one brother refused to make room and move his legs, another brother promptly vomited all over his shoes.

Customs cleared us in a flash.

Some feel differently about the passing of J. L. Hudson's from the landscape of Detroit.

Vern Cope, a real estate agent now living in Kingsville who worked in the men's clothing department in the store's last years, doesn't mourn its death.

"If it had been a great store right up until yesterday then, yes, I would feel badly, but it's been vacant for years—it's been on the blocks."

Still, Cope has a soft spot for the store with chandeliered ceilings, firework shows, a store that used to drape the world's largest U.S. flag over its exterior.

"Yes, it was the finest I'd ever been in." [Feb. 7, 1997]

Everyone Knew...

[Parke Davis Pharmaceuticals]

EVERYBODY IN THE NEIGHBOURHOOD KNEW WHAT WAS UP. These little black panel trucks would run up and down the streets, stopping at houses. They'd see the driver jump out, reach into the truck for an empty gallon jug.

They'd see the smiling housewife at the screen door handing the driver a full jug, and taking the empty from him. She'd wave goodbye and say, "See you next month!"

Every month the same. Driver and housewife.

And the cheques would roll in to these happy housewives.

This mysterious program was run by Parke, Davis and Company, then situated at the corner of Walker Road and Riverside Drive.

The program, which ran from about 1929 to 1935, involved collecting jugs of urine from pregnant women.

With the extra money, these women were able to cover hospital costs involved in having these babies.

Eighty-year-old Bill Miles recalls these transactions vividly. He lived in the Hickory Road area, and saw the Parke, Davis people coming and going.

"We always knew when a woman was pregnant . . . We'd see them (Parke, Davis) coming. We also knew about a (new) pregnancy when our moms would suddenly announce to us when we were ready to throw out the newspapers: 'Save those newspapers for Mrs. So-and-So down the road!'

"We knew what that meant—we had to save the papers to cover the bedsheets at the time of delivery . . ."

A 40-year veteran of Wyeth, a rival pharmaceutical company in Windsor, also remembers hearing about these panel trucks.

What did they use the urine for? To produce a hormonal replacement drug for women.

This pharmaceutical company worker, who prefers to remain anonymous, knew that's what these jugs of urine were being used for because Wyeth's sister company in St. Laurent, Quebec was doing something similar.

"But unlike Parke, Davis, this company near Montreal—it was called Ayerst, McKenna and Harrison—had a horse farm and they'd use the urine from pregnant mares—they didn't use human urine!"

The urine was reduced to a salt residue.

Parke, Davis was established in Windsor in 1890. Interestingly enough, its first experimental studies conducted here were with respect to prevention and cure of widespread animal diseases such as hog cholera, sheep scab, tuberculosis, tetanus, and anthrax.

With respect to the urine collection, Parke, Davis discontinued the practice when they discovered "the women were diluting the jugs with tap water."

This former Wyeth manager has his own stories about pharmaceutical companies based here. He figures Walkerville was put on the map—not entirely because of Hiram Walker and Sons—but because of Wyeth's wartime efforts to help the troops.

Millions of "V-packs" were shipped to barracks and to the front during the Second World War.

Victory Packs? Like Victory Bonds?

Not exactly.

These tiny packages—labeled with the manufacturer's offices in Walkerville, Ont., Canada—were first spotted by this gentleman during the war when he stepped inside a guard house at one of the Canadian bases. He spotted the name "Walkerville." Being from Windsor, he couldn't help but be drawn to the name. His inquiry resulted in this knowledge: These V-packs were for the treatment of venereal disease. The kit included swabs and ointment tubes.

"Of course, I never used one of them," this man told me, laughing.

"As a matter of fact, I don't know of anyone who did use one, but they were there along with supplies of condoms.

"And you could go in there and pop a few of those in your pocket if you thought things were going to be good for you that night," he said. [Nov. 16, 2001]

September 11th

[Michael Nosanchuk]

THE DAY WAS SEPTEMBER 11TH. He hid in the cellar and could hear the search parties above and after what seemed an eternity, he decided to crawl out.

"I decided to crawl out . . . and go into the darkness like a wild animal. I felt I was walking on dead bodies. . . . Where should I go?"

He's not talking about New York, nor the World Trade Center. He is not remembering the events of Sept. 11, 2001. Rather, it's about the events of Sept. 11, 1942.

It is the 59th anniversary of the massacre of the Jews in the ghetto in Stolin, located in what was once called "White Russia."

The words are those of Michael Nosanchuk, a man who for years ran the Prince Road convenience store. He died in 1984. His memories of these horrifying events of six decades ago have just surfaced in a memoir that has remained virtually unknown all these years.

"We only just got it three weeks ago and we've had it translated from the Yiddish," said Judge Saul Nosanchuk, Michael's nephew.

The memoir was probably written in the displaced-persons camps in Germany right after the fall of Berlin.

Michael Nosanchuk had joined with the partisans and later the Red Army, to drive back the German armies.

In another holograph—a letter written to Saul's father—he described it thus: "I was on the front lines outside of Warsaw and I ended in the darkness of Berlin. I took revenge for our innocent spilled blood. But the great wound will not heal."

On the eve of Rosh Hashanah, Sept. 11, 1942, the German SS prepared open graves for the 7,000 Jews they ordered to strip naked. They then forced the Jews to lie down in the graves and promptly and coldly machine-gunned them down.

"I will never forget the last night. . . . I was with my parents until three o'clock in the morning. We said goodbye, we kissed and cried. . . . Father recited Kaddish. Mother washed and put on the nicest dress she had, preparing herself for death. They sent me out of the house.

"At the moment I could not believe the words spoken by my parents. . . . To say goodbye—to kiss your beautiful mother and father and family for the last time, knowing that in hours we would all be dead. They wanted so much for me to remain alive."

Later he would write to Saul's father in Windsor: "A thousand times I cursed that moment when I left. I often wished that I had lain down with them and embraced them, as all the martyrs did. . . ."

Michael hid in the cellar for 18 days after the slaughter. Finally he ventured out: "I felt I was walking on dead bodies. . . ."

From that point, Michael was on the run, first joining the partisans, then the Red Army. After the war he ended up in a displaced-persons camp, then came to Canada.

Saul remembers that day well. It was August 1947. Saul was 13. He stood with his parents at the Windsor station waiting for Michael Nosanchuk's train to pull in.

Finally, Saul's uncle stepped off the train. His eyes were bright and hopeful and relieved that finally the ordeal of Europe—the war, the running and the hiding from the Nazis and the horrible reality of having lost parents to the violence and hate—was over.

"Why so glum?" he demanded, as he stared at his distraught brother, whom he had not seen for years.

"Where's Michael?" he asked, referring to his 10-year-old nephew who was named after him.

The family was silent. Saul's brother had died only three weeks before in a swimming accident at Colchester.

In the arms of Saul's uncle was an accordion he had brought with him from Europe to give to the young nephew who was named after him.

Here I am 54 years later, talking to Saul about how his uncle—then 36—moved into their house on Elsmere.

"We shared a room—he took my brother's bed and there we were, me a 13-year-old boy and him, in his 30s, sleeping like brothers."

Two months ago, Saul and his nephew Murray Nosanchuk (Michael's son) were to make a pilgrimage to White Russia to the site of that brutal murder of their family.

Sept. 11, 2001 put an end to that. [Nov. 2, 2001]

Garage Sale Find

[Father Edward William Allor]

AN OLD TRUNK AT A GARAGE SALE. A rusted lock that took some force to break open. The start of a search.

The search for a man from Detroit who worked at Ford's Highland Park plant. His story is contained, in part, in an 88-year-old letter from Harry Hudson, this man's former boss and friend, who sailed to England with Henry Ford's right-hand man, Charles E. Sorensen.

Hudson's letter sent from England to this Detroit gentleman speaks about Ford's expansion over there, and how it had finally switched over from assembly operation to manufacturing.

This old friend from Detroit had just taken over from Hudson as a foreman in the radiator department at the Highland Park plant. But he wouldn't stay there. Instead he would make his way across the river to Canada to become a Basilian priest, spending most of his life on this side, serving various parishes, including Assumption and Amherstburg's St. John the Baptist.

Indeed, that's where this trunk came from. It had been tossed out in a parish garage sale.

This man—Father Edward William Allor—had served this parish church on a number of occasions. The last time was in 1972, two years before his death.

Allor was there off and on during the '40s, '50s and '60s. He was a priest with an obsession with clocks, pieces of which were found with the trunk. There was also a photograph of Allor, taken by Charles White in Detroit. There was his diploma in philosophy from the University of Western Ontario, then the granting institution for Assumption College.

Who was this priest? That's exactly what Sandra Di Pasquale wants to know. She's the one who brought home this trunk. She'd always wanted something like this as a coffee table for her rec room. Her husband, Frank, hauled the case downstairs and tried to jimmy the lock to get at the contents inside.

After failing, he telephoned his friend, Mark Restoule, for

assistance, and the two pried open the case. There inside, of course, was this handwritten letter postmarked Aug. 22, 1913 from England, and addressed to Ed Allor who at the time lived at 1015 Harper Ave. in Detroit.

It became the source of this search.

Restoule, who fancies such old artifacts, immediately recognized the historical significance of this correspondence. He understood that this little-known priest was a confidante of Hudson. Allor's old boss is very candid about Ford's planned expansion, about details of its labour problems. We learn too that Ford has patented some sort of device created by Allor.

There are also references to Sorensen travelling to Ireland and France to expand operations. This, Allor is told, must be kept quiet.

The significance of such a letter? Restoule feels it provides us an intimate glimpse into the first moves Ford made to expand its manufacturing operations beyond the North American borders.

What about Allor? He didn't stay long with the car company. Apparently the Ford family pleaded with him to stay. But Allor crossed over to Windsor instead, where he enrolled at Assumption, then entered the Basilians in 1917. Six years later, he was ordained.

The first church this Michigan-born priest was assigned to was Assumption. In 1926 he was was made its pastor, and remained there till 1937. Allor would return to Assumption on three other occasions. He was also pastor at St. Anne's in Detroit.

But who was this man, whom his bishop described as "a model parish priest?" A nephew of his recalls the old priest pointing skyward to the "A" on the Ambassador Bridge and remarking, "I was up there!"

As an engineer? Steeplejack? Prankster? Angel?

Who knows. [Aug. 28, 2001]

Little Miss Chicago

[Herbert M. Lee]

TWO BOYS STOOD ON THE PLATFORM waiting for the Grand Trunk Western out of Chicago. It was just after the American Thanksgiving. They could see the cars rounding the bend. George was 13. His brother, John, two years older. They were waiting for their father—Herbert M. Lee—to return from the Chicago International Livestock Exposition. And as the train rumbled in, and came to a halt, they waited and watched while the boxcar was shunted free.

Their father was riding with his prize-winning sheep. Lincolns. He rode with them in the windy wooden boxcars with a steel roof. He slept on a straw mattress on a makeshift deck, bundled up in sweaters and coats. He read by the lamplight of a coal oil lantern.

Eleven hours it took to get down to Chicago from Highgate, Ont. He'd leave at night and arrive the next day. It was worth it. His sheep won in just about every class. Red ribbons were stuffed in a suitcase. John and George knew that.

Their father shepherded his sheep to agricultural fairs all over Ontario and the U.S., and the boys would marvel at the ribbons, and fall over themselves petitioning him to tell them all about it.

This time, things were different. Their father was returning from Chicago. It was 1935. This time the boys knew all about what had happened in Chicago.

A reporter from *The Windsor Daily Star* had stopped by Leeland Farms. Someone else had called from the *Chatham Daily News*.

All the talk was about "Little Miss Chicago." A lamb born out of lambing season at the Chicago International Exposition. An unusual event, and one that brought sheep farmers and livestock specialists from far and wide to check out this lamb. The Chicago papers had christened the animal "Little Miss Chicago." Its cute little face adorned the front pages. It was the talk of the town.

I'm told this story by John, now 82, who still lives in Highgate. Still lives on his childhood farm. Still sleeps in the bedroom he slept in as a kid. Little has changed. Like his father, he, too, became a sheep farmer. And like his father, he, too, is just as passionate about raising sheep.

Up until just a few years ago, the two brothers continued the tradition. A serious tradition. Serious enough that one of the small things Herbert Lee had taught his boys was a Latin poem from Virgil.

A poem? Indeed.

One that John still knows by heart.

If wool be thy care, let not thy cattle go
Where bushes are, where burrs and thistles grow
Neither in too rank a pasture let them feed
And of the purest white select they breed

John will tell you his father believed strongly in the fundamentals of livestock breeding, and that included memorizing this poem.

"Not only the poem," John added, "but what it meant."

The Lees have raised sheep since 1889. They first took them down to show at the Chicago Exposition in 1910, and ceased doing this in 1971 when foot and mouth disease broke out in Alberta, thereby barring all cloven hoofed animals from entry into the U.S. from Canada.

Leeland Farm is a quiet place these days. The sheep are long gone. The barns are empty tombs. And the baby monitor in John's bedroom remains there, a reminder of when he kept a close ear to the sounds of the ewes giving birth, and would rise from his bed and head out to the barn.

Today, his routine is different. John slips into his car in the morning and heads to the coffee shop on the main drag of Highgate. There he engages in the talk of the town. The local gossip. The stories circulating about farmers, and the land, and what's been in the paper or on the television news. Last night's hockey game.

But lodged in his memory—and his heart—are those days as a young man when he followed in his father's footsteps and rode the rails to the Chicago fair, first stopping at the Royal Winter Fair.

Riding the rails with 30 or more sheep.

"It must've smelled terribly," I suggest.

"Well, it smelled of sheep," he says "But you know once you got to the windy city, the wind would just blow it right off you . . ." [Nov. 27, 2002]

Church Suppers & Rebels

Angels With Dirty Faces

[Father Gerald Quenneville]

HUNDREDS OF ALTAR BOYS SCRAMBLED ONTO TRAINS from all over the London Diocese to make their way to London to hear this quiet-spoken Italian priest encourage them to begin thinking about being priests. A nice idea. The bishop's idea.

This story is really Father Gerald Quenneville's. He shared this with Pam Bowsher, a colleague from the *Star*. She, in turn, passed it on to me. It's a tale of how during the late '50s this youthful, good-looking priest arrived at the Windsor train station to join with altar boys from his parish. The kids dutifully waited on the platform—all dressed in starched white surplices and frayed black cassocks. The look on the faces of their mothers immediately telegraphed the message that something was awry.

Their eyes didn't speak of forlorn farewell. The smiles were more self-satisfied smirks. They knew their kids.

And what folly that these men of the church—with absolutely no experience caring for children—would actually believe they could maintain order among hundreds of healthy, active kids on a train ride to London without a woman's help.

Good luck. And God forgive them.

By Belle River, the neatly packaged lunches the moms had made for their angelic boys had been pillaged.

By Tilbury, all the water in the train had been drained, and the toilets were out of order.

By St. Thomas, the train crew was ready for mutiny, as altar boys did 100-yard dashes up and down the cars.

A big mistake, mouthed a silent Father Quenneville whom I imagine sunk his head into his hands in despair.

The idea upon arrival was to have the kids parade up Richmond to St. Peter's Basilica on Dufferin.

About a 20-minute march. You might assume it ought to have been orderly, pious, joyous.

Instead many of the kids broke lines, and bolted for the shops, raiding comic book stores, candy outlets, toy shops.

The next morning the *London Free Press* ran a front-page picture of one altar boy, minus the halo, with a fat cigar stuffed in his mouth.

Finally, upon reaching their destination, the kids filed into lines with a lot of venomous and frustrated coaxing from many of the priests who, I'm sure, were now having serious doubts about their vocation.

The boys assembled at the cathedral, standing on the newly mown lawn, and straining to hear this kindly old priest whose voice carried maybe only two or three rows. It didn't take long for this momentary decorum to erupt in bedlam as boys began to engage in a war of tossing mounds of grass clippings at one another. The boys also yanked down the collars of other unsuspecting altar boys in front of them, and jammed grass down their backsides.

This was not a moment of glory for Holy Mother Church.

This was the work of the devil.

And oh my Lord, a collective moan among the priests was heard: There would be confessions droning on all over the diocese from altar boys. Every confession the same.

Bless me Father, for I have sinned . . . I misbehaved in front of a holy priest from Rome . . .

An event these diocesan priests would have preferred to forget.

It wasn't long before altar boys were herded back onto the trains.

This time, however, Father Quenneville, with brows furrowed and his dark piercing eyes flashing in anger, positioned himself at the front of the train car carrying his altar boys. He removed his belt, and then warned the boys in no uncertain terms that if one of them stepped out of line, he'd strap them.

When the kids arrived back in Windsor, they ran into the waiting arms of their moms, and pointed back at Father Quenneville, declaring how Father had threatened to strap them. That didn't sit well with the moms.

But Father Quenneville didn't wait around to answer questions.

Instead, he retreated like a defeated Confederate soldier to the rectory. He threw himself down on the floor in the living room.

A fellow priest stood over him.

"What's wrong?" he implored.

"Never mind," replied a beaten Father Quenneville. "Get me a drink, fast." [Aug. 19, 1998]

They Call Him Father

[Rev. Paul Charbonneau]

THEY CALL HIM FATHER. As I sit across from him in a modest office on the site of an old Windsor nightclub, I can hear men talking in the adjacent room. The refrain is unmistakable. Like schoolboys, followers, adherents, they say, "Well, Father says . . ."

This man, leaning back in a swivel chair and chomping on a fat El Producto cigar, is the enigmatic founder of Brentwood—Rev. Paul Charbonneau. The one who breathes the fires of damnation into the souls of the men and women who come to see him. He snuffs out their bravado. Makes then face facts. Makes them accountable. Makes them start respecting life.

Charbonneau, who turns 76 in July, is someone with the authority of Moses. An authority so large it has driven converts to snitch on each other if they catch one of their kind stepping into a bar.

He's a man who operates on self-confidence, determination, steadfast will. Some will say, correctly, his bite is worse than his bark.

Charbonneau sees himself differently. Portrays himself as a softie, a compassionate individual, someone eager to listen, ready to help.

In a way, he's right. There's no denying, however, that ever-present, feisty, gruff side that warns you to never test this man, never to cross him. You know from the beginning that his penetrating eyes will challenge and vex you into focusing on the world differently.

With the exception of a brief period after his official retirement four years ago, Charbonneau has been at the helm of Brentwood Recovery Home from day one, in 1964. It wasn't until 1984 that he moved the operation to the former Elmwood Casino nightspot.

It wasn't easy in the beginning. For years, as a parish priest, serving parishes in Windsor, Tecumseh and Emeryville, he was forced to divide his time between tending to his flock and helping alcoholics.

Misery among his own congregation rarely escaped him. It might be a wife who had endured the abuse of a drunken husband, or a family down and out because a father had squandered all his earnings on poker or drink.

Charbonneau detected it instantly. Especially that "look" in the face of a distraught wife.

He recognized his own mother's face when his father would launch into drunken rages. Charbonneau couldn't sit back in the rectory, and rationalize, "God will take care of it all." That wasn't good enough. He made a point of confronting those wives, offering help. It made it easier for them when he confessed the fierce grip alcoholism had on his own family.

"I came from a home with lots of anger, sadness, hurt and confusion . . . I grew up pretty tough, and not a lot of priests had this . . ."

The breakthrough for Charbonneau in those early days was speaking to the husbands. Often he was ordered out of the house. Sometimes fists were raised. It wasn't uncommon for Charbonneau to put up his dukes, and challenge the husbands to step outside.

"I wasn't afraid of anybody . . . Even those twice my size . . . I learned early that it's all bluff with the alcoholic . . . They're so full of guilt and shame."

Friday, this LaSalle born priest celebrates 50 years as a priest.

In some ways Charbonneau hasn't changed. Same routine. Still up at 4:45 A.M. Drives in every day from Harrow where he resides. At his desk at 6:30 A.M. Works till 4:00 P.M. Manages on about six hours sleep.

"I read something when I was 12 that we spent one third of our life in bed . . . I thought, 'That'll *never* happen to me.'"

It didn't.

Charbonneau's like a threshing machine that never stops. Looking back, he acknowledges that in the seminary he was plagued with doubts about continuing.

"I hated studying . . . I just wanted to get out there and live . . ."

That's his gift—rejoicing in life, in getting to know *his* people.

"That's what it was like for a priest years ago. He knew everybody. Made a point of it. Kept in touch.

"But I'm a better priest today than I ever was. Much more grateful and content within myself. My faith is stronger. I hope that's not because of old age." [May 15, 1998]

Blessed Are The Poor

[Mother Teresa]

WHEN I HEARD THAT MOTHER TERESA would be beatified this weekend in Rome, I thought back to those "holy cards" of saints the nuns used to hand out at school. I also recalled pestering the nuns and the priests with the same question: Why aren't there any modern saints?

We wanted to know why there weren't any strolling about in the sunlight, breathing the same air we breathed?

It's hard to believe we now have one.

Mother Teresa—that diminutive four-foot-eleven nun, who set up a mission some 22 years ago in the streets of Detroit's Cass Corridor, will be elevated to a status just one notch below sainthood.

It's now only a matter of time before she'll be Saint Teresa of Calcutta.

Mother Teresa made a couple of visits to Detroit, and on one of those occasions I got to talk to her in the basement of what was then called St. Agnes Catholic Church (now Martyrs of Uganda Church) on Rosa Parks Boulevard. She was there to visit her sisters from the Missionaries of Charity.

Some 1,500 had crowded into the worn oak pews of that sweltering sanctuary to mark the opening of her mission, an oasis to help the homeless mothers, the destitute, the prostitutes, anyone on the run, anyone in need.

Mother Teresa made it clear that the only thing she asked for in return for serving these people a hot meal or providing them a clean place to stay was that they say grace before meals and prayers before they went to bed.

Nothing more.

No one would be turned away.

And these indigent men, women and children returned daily. They were polite, full of gratitude. Their eyes shone with buoyant optimism and hope, the spirit and humanity Mother Teresa had offered to millions around the world. It swarmed in the eyes of those ravaged souls who lived on the fringe—the victims of poverty, crime, drug abuse.

I can't forget that night when I met Mother Teresa and followed her down to the basement just before the service ended. It was there that I was to interview her.

Organizers had arranged a luncheon of sandwiches, cakes and coffee, but when Mother Teresa surveyed the sea of trays loaded with food, she immediately summoned a smiling and admiring woman wearing an apron.

"What is this?" Mother Teresa asked.

The woman, bursting with pride at the bountiful assortment of food, said it was for the invited guests upstairs in the church.

"No," said Mother Teresa, shaking her head and wagging a bony finger, "Pack it up!"

"Excuse me?" said the bewildered organizer from the Catholic Women's League.

"Pack up everything before they come downstairs!"

"But . . . but . . . they're expecting . . ."

"Pack it up, now!" repeated an emphatic Mother Teresa. "Give it to the poor! The people up there don't need it—the people in this neighbourhood need it more . . . Box it up and save it for them!"

The woman rushed back to the others. At first, she may not have believed Mother Teresa was serious. Perhaps she worried about angering the bishop. In any case, she gathered up others to help. I saw them nervously repackaging everything and storing it away in the kitchen.

Then I stood back and studied the panic in the faces of those upstairs who had suddenly arrived in the basement where the tables had been cleared.

One man—obviously in charge—swept into the kitchen demanding to know why nothing had been set up yet.

And when it was explained to him, he wheeled about in the direction of Mother Teresa, who was now talking to the guests filing into the church basement.

Mother Teresa's behaviour wasn't for the benefit of Detroit's TV crews and photographers. They were still upstairs. I was the only one from the media there. She certainly didn't do it for me. It was instinct. It was in keeping with who she was, and what she stood for. She recognized the incongruity of launching a mission for the poor, and celebrating this by feeding those who could well afford to pay for their meal.

The next day at St. Agnes's soup kitchen, the poor feasted on the delicate sandwiches and donuts that had been intended for Detroit's mayor, the governor of Michigan, the corporate bigwigs and the city's clergy.

No one was thinking of sainthood then. The poor were merely hungry. The bigwigs were merely busy. Mother Teresa was merely herself. [Oct. 16, 2003]

The Barnyard Intellectual

[Father Stan Murphy]

YOU WOULD NEVER HAVE BELIEVED THIS FELLOW. This quiet, unassuming Catholic priest whom I'd met nervously tapping an index finger at a kitchen table in a friend's house having tea. He was there for a child's birthday party. Or maybe it was around Christmas. Just passing the time away.

An ordinary cleric. A bit of a hayseed. The ruralness of a farm near Woodslee, where he was raised, still clinging to him.

You would never have believed him.

The barnyard intellectual.

The talk with him would start and it would circle around family and kids and jobs, then suddenly it would take off in another direction, and now we were tackling literature and philosophy and church doctrine.

That man was Father Stan Murphy, the one who started the Christian Culture Series in 1934 in a move to bring culture to Windsor. He wrote letters all over the world, inviting speakers—major philosophers, writers, musicians—to Windsor. The funny thing is they agreed. They came here. And Father Stan filled the old Capitol Theatre downtown. He got the best.

At his urgings, he also managed to lure Marshall McLuhan and Wyndham Lewis to teach at Assumption University.

The sad thing about Father Murphy, I think, is that he never got to tell the stories behind all these people. He knew so many over the years, having fostered relationships with some of the greatest thinkers of the 20th century.

The archives at Assumption demonstrate this clearly.

Thanks to Michael Power, a Windsor-born writer and archivist who was responsible for setting up those archives, and in particular, the papers of Father Murphy, we can glimpse a little of this man's achievements.

Now, the story of the Christian Culture Award, a prize Father Stan started in 1941 to honour a distinguished person who has contributed greatly to the furtherance of Christian ideas in art, literature, philosophy or science, is documented in yet another book by Power published by Assumption University.

Power, who now lives in Trenton, Ont., has compiled short biographies of the recipients of the Christian Culture Award. These include such individuals as Sigrid Undset, a Norwegian novelist and short story writer who won the Nobel Prize, Henry Ford II, Jean Vanier, Jean Chretien, the late Paul Martin and his son, Paul Martin Jr.

As I scanned through Power's book, I thought about some of the people behind the award. Notably the stories behind these individuals.

Two amusing tales in particular come to mind.

There's one of William Kurelek, who was one of this country's most prolific narrative painters. The story about him is that he made a phone call to W.O. Mitchell, writer-in-residence at the University of Windsor, and asked if he might illustrate *Who Has Seen The Wind*. Mitchell shrugged. He was obviously reticent about letting some hack take on this job.

And so, Kurelek—feeling a little chastised—offered to let him see some of his pictures to give Mitchell an idea of what he could do. The curmudgeonly writer from Alberta, who told me this story, reluctantly agreed to interrupt his busy schedule and thumb through what he anticipated to be boring examples of amateur pictures.

The fact is Mitchell *did* know Kurelek, and knew his art well, but the way Kurelek pronounced his name wasn't the way Mitchell pronounced it.

And so, he didn't recognize him.

But as soon as Kurelek sat down and opened up a portfolio, Mitchell immediately recognized the artist's style.

"Oh, you're Bill *Kurelek!*" Mitchell roared when he saw the pictures in his office.

"You're *that* Kurelek!" he repeated.

Kurelek nodded, but then corrected him on how the name should be pronounced.

Now Mitchell was embarrassed.

The two struck a deal right there. The book was finally published with the artist's pictures and Mitchell's words.

Another story concerns the rather pensive and sober broadcaster Roy Bonisteel, best remembered for his award-winning Man Alive television series. He was given the award in 1982. Here was a man who exuded a seriousness about spirituality. Yet when I went to visit him near Belleville where he lived, I found him lolling about in a room full of old-fashioned pinball machines, a passion of his. He seemed a little embarrassed that I had caught him there at something so frivolous, but Bonisteel shrugged and said, "What the Hell! I'm only human!" [January 23, 2002]

Cut From The Cloth Of A Saint

[Rev. Mike Dalton]

"THIS IS GENE," CAME THE VOICE OVER THE PHONE in that unmistakable drawl.

Gene Whelan. The hayseed Socrates. Former agriculture minister in Pierre Trudeau's cabinet. He was telephoning to tell me he had stopped in at the 100th birthday celebration for Rev. Mike Dalton, the old soldier who landed at Normandy on D-Day with Canadian troops. I'm talking about the old army padre who said mass for thousands of battle-worn men from atop his jeep. The padre whose war uniform still hangs in his nursing home room at Sacred Heart Villa in Courtland, where he has lived for several years. The padre whose story I write every year because it was a promise I made him. A priest for 70 years. The one who warned me that if his birthday did come along, and he was still alive, fine, but if he didn't survive, the party should go on without him.

This past weekend, Dalton was there in all his glory and very much alive, clutching the hands of some 250 former parishioners, dignitaries and colleagues.

Gene was feeling good because the first thing the bright-eyed Dalton, sitting in his wheelchair, remarked to him was: "I remember you—you were my minister of agriculture!" He also recalled having celebrated Gene's marriage at the church in Kingsville 42 years ago.

Dalton's story is a good news one at a time when the church is ravaged and beseiged by scandal. He was a down-to-earth priest who cared about the people he served. There's a story about him that after his retirement and being dispatched to Ingersoll, he made a point of knocking on every parishioner's door. Fifteen hundred church members. He saw each and every one of them, and some hadn't seen a priest on their doorstep in 40 years.

That was the kind of man he was. A grassroots priest, cut from the cloth of a saint. Someone who did the job. Someone who believed in people and doing good.

There are photographs in our files at the *Windsor Star* showing him on D-Day with the troops. He ignored each and every order issued to him about staying put and staying well behind the line of fire. Instead, the old soldier charged ahead, wanting to be where he was needed. And that was at the front in the midst of battle, where he could console the soldiers, where he could hear their confessions, offer them communion, or even just pat them on the shoulder and urge them to persevere.

Dalton's memory of that time is vivid. He can't forget the young men wild with fear, "cracking up and crying like babies."

Gene knew the old priest as a bit of a joker and can remember one election during the 1960s when Mike Pearson was struggling to hold off the Tory war horse John Diefenbaker.

"We were mainstreeting in Kingsville," Gene said, "and I saw Father Mike standing all alone in front of the church."

The next thing he knew, Pearson had crossed the road to talk with the priest. The two were sharing a good laugh over how they both had the same first name. At that point, Dalton snapped his fingers and out poured a dozen or more altar boys. Pearson engaged them in conversation and asked one boy, "What's your name son?"

"Mike," the boy shot back.

Mike Pearson laughed at the coincidence that now he was standing with two others that shared the same first name.

"And your name, son?" he said to another.

"Mike."

Pearson laughed again.

He went down the line, and one by one—just as Dalton had privately instructed—each boy, without batting an eye, told the prime minister his name was Mike.

Dalton's practical joke.

After he hung up the phone, I wondered why Gene Whelan was telling me this story and why he bothered to call. Was it because it's something special for someone to reach 100? Sure, that's got to be part of it, but there's something more here. Dalton was a man of destiny and purpose. This is to be respected and admired. He often thought of himself as lucky. Twice his jeep in the midst of battle was hit with shrapnel and he walked away without a scratch.

There was a reason he survived.

There was a reason he reached 100. [May 8, 2002]

The Preacher And The Hockey Player

[Rev. Ken Jaggs & Tim Horton]

WHEN THEY WERE BOYS IN COCHRANE, ONT., their backyards faced one another. They played on the same hockey team. They were rough and tumble teenagers with fierce tempers and didn't tolerate nonsense on the ice. And if challenged, they'd think nothing of doing battle. When they became men, one went into the priesthood, the other into the NHL. They remained friends all their lives.

The other day, Rev. Ken Jaggs, an Anglican priest whose parish is St. George's in old Walkerville, was remembering his old buddy. It's something he doesn't let go easily because while it may have something to do with his love of the game of hockey, it's also because his friend's name—it seems—is on nearly every other corner of nearly every town in Canada.

His buddy was Tim Horton, who died in February 1974 while driving home from a Buffalo Sabres game. He is best remembered, however, as one of the great Toronto Maple Leafs players who started with the team in 1952 and was traded in 1970 to the New York Rangers. A year later, Horton was sent to the Pittsburgh Penguins. In 1972, Buffalo picked him up.

Of course you still get those incredulous looks from some who don't quite believe it when you say the donut chain was started by this hockey great. Some—especially younger people—don't even know Horton was a hockey player. But this Cochrane-born player, who dallied a bit in a hamburger chain, opened his first store in Hamilton, Ontario in 1964. A year later, he found a partner who invested $10,000 into the business. Upon his death, this partner offered the hockey player's widow a million dollars for the chain that by this time had expanded to some 40 stores.

In a coffee shop last week, Jaggs got around to talking about Horton and the time they played on the same high school hockey team. He said he had never met anyone so "strong" as Horton.

"He used to pick up huge boulders and hold them up over his head. You know, he never initiated a fight."

But Jaggs remembers one fight back then when someone made an ugly remark to Horton, and he "belted this fellow and he went down like a rock."

More often than not, Horton would come to the rescue of his teammates, sometimes "picking them up, grabbing them like a bear around their waist," and separating them from the fight.

"He was so strong—and his neck was as wide as a thigh."

When Horton went off to St. Michael's in Toronto and played for its major Junior A club, Jaggs' family moved to Preston.

"I played for the Junior B team in Cambridge." Jaggs also joined the high school team. "I was a bit of a mixer—I wasn't afraid to hit." ·

In the final game for the provincial high school championship against a team from Weston, near Toronto, Jaggs was thrown out of the game for fighting. That year the team from Weston was coached by Toronto Maple Leafs goaltender Turk Broda. Also on that team was Billy Harris, who later would join the Leafs.

"I saw Tim play back then whenever St. Mike's was in Galt. Terry Sawchuk was playing with the Galt Red Wings back then."

The friendship grew between Jaggs and Horton during the summer months of 1945 when the two weeded gardens in the Holland Marshes outside of Toronto.

"We really bonded then," said Jaggs.

Their friendship even developed its own superstition, at least on the part of Horton, who believed obsessively that his buddy could help the Leafs win. "It seemed every time I went to watch him, the Leafs would win," says Jaggs, who was lured by Horton to Maple Leaf Gardens whenever there was a critical game. Jaggs would dutifully pack up and head for Toronto, stay with his friend, and then return home to Windsor the next day.

And the Leafs would always win.

And whenever the Leafs were in Detroit, they'd trounce the Wings—providing the Anglican cleric was there. Jaggs rarely missed a game. He had no choice. Horton demanded it. Then again, he didn't mind. In those teen years, like Horton, Jaggs thought of nothing else but becoming a hockey player, a star like his buddy. Being a priest was the furthest from his mind. Up until a few years ago, Jaggs still played recreational hockey.

The dream was still in his bones. [Nov. 22, 2005]

Fighters, Rink Rats, Hockey Dads, Ballplayers . . .

The Man Who Ate Lightbulbs

[Abdullah The Butcher aka Larry Shreve]

HE CRUNCHED UP LIGHT BULBS IN HIS TEETH, swallowed snakes, chewed up reams of newspaper, and gobbled the heads off fish. He chased fighters into jeering crowds and smashed chairs over terrified opponents. He screamed and yelled and threw temper tantrums in the ring. Anything to get attention. Anything to get the crowds back the next night in arenas all over North America.

Part of the act for this 400-pound wrestler, Abdullah The Butcher, was pretending he couldn't speak English. In front of TV cameras, he'd stutter moronically with a fake accent, repeating two words, "Me beat! Me beat! Me beat!"

If someone recognized him from Windsor's McDougall Avenue, where he grew up, and called him "Larry Shreve," he'd rage and pound his chest in fierce denial, claiming, "No, Abdullah! Abdullah!"

I got hold of this character, whose age is a mystery because web sites offer differing birth dates for him. I telephoned him in Atlanta, Georgia where he operates a restaurant called Abdullah The Butcher's House of Ribs. I called because at the 2nd Annual Fight Night at the Coboto Club, he is being honoured. It's part of a week-long celebration called the McDougall Street Reunion, organized by Northstar Cultural Community Centre.

Abdullah—clearly in his mid-60s—grew up in that neighbour-hood but left Windsor to pursue a wrestling career.

In those 47 years in the ring, he's battered the likes of such legends as The Sheik, Dusty Rhodes and Bobo Brazil.

"I've fought them all," Abdullah boasts.

True enough. He has.

Abdullah made his mark in the ring alongside Andre The Giant and Bruiser Brody.

Steve Slagle in *Ring Chronicle* wrote: "Of the dozens of blood-thirsty, psychotic personalities our sport has been home to, few can rival the sheer violence, insanity and chaos created by the 'Madman from the Sudan,' Abdullah the Butcher."

For five decades, he said, this man has bloodied and battered his opponents "with a vengeance like few others in the history of the business." Slagle describes Abdullah's unscientific fighting style as "simplistic and barbaric," and the model for the generations of "wildmen" that followed.

Is that true?

"I had to do something different," Abdullah told me over the phone. Abdullah, a son of a Ford Motor Company factory worker, left Patterson Collegiate to sell papers, start his own janitorial service and operate a clothing store on Wyandotte Street.

When he speaks about those years, he talks about "wrassling," a term often used by old time wrestlers.

A Detroit promoter spotted him and liked his style, and at 19 he became a regular in the ring.

"When they saw me wrassle, they said I fought like a wild man."

It meant a name change. At first it was Zeras Amala. From time to time, it changed to Pussycat Pikens, Wildman from the Sudan, Blade Bordeaux, but the name that stuck was Abdullah the Butcher. This was the result of a riot he started in a Seattle arena in 1965.

Abdullah's method in the ring was to karate chop his opponents in the neck. He also enacted a swift and effective dropkick.

But what caught everyone's attention was his outrageous behaviour in the ring. "I'd freak out. I'd eat a snake, or dog, or raw fish, anything."

Including light bulbs.

He let me in on how he managed to accomplish this last trick. Abdullah applied vaseline to his lips and inside his mouth.

"The average person doesn't know that when you eat a light bulb and chew it with your teeth, it is ground to a powder. And that powder will stick to the vaseline, and so when the fight was over, I'd scoop out the (ground) glass inside my mouth with my finger."

The point of it was to garner attention, and bring the crowds back. Abdullah did just that. He has tallied up a list of championship bouts, but a triumphant moment occurred in 1972 in Montreal when a throng of 26,000 turned out to witness the beating he put on Johnny Rougeau.

"As an entertainer, if you do everything the same, you're nothing," he said.

Abdullah returns to Windsor from time to time, because he still owns real estate in the city. But he has settled in Atlanta and runs a rib restaurant. He hasn't given up fighting.

"I still fight," he said.

As Slagle put it, Abdullah's focus has always been the same: ". . . violence, mayhem and shocking the fans." [Aug. 3, 2006]

A Tall Right Hander

[Fergie Jenkins]

HE DIDN'T MISS TOO MANY TIMES. He certainly never broke any windows. He was there day after day, this big lanky kid, throwing balls on the street in front of his house. Day after day. Summer after summer. Firing balls like there was no tomorrow. The baseballs rising and falling at a tremendous speed and occasionally ricocheting off a glove and maybe hitting the wall of his home on Adelaide Street here.

The house still sits there. A modest aluminum-sided home at 213 Adelaide South in Chatham, Ont. Today there's a For Sale sign lodged in the front lawn. And when people pass by they talk. This was the childhood home of baseball legend Ferguson Jenkins. It is selling for $72,900. The house in which the former six-foot-five Chicago Cubs pitcher lived from the age of seven.

Bonnie Martin, a former business teacher at St. Clair College, and cousin to Fergie, is organizing a committee to see if the house can be bought and turned into a museum.

"I'm not sure what we're going to do. I only just found out about the house going up for sale, but something should be done to preserve this place, because this is history."

Martin remembers that home well.

"I was over there all the time," she said. "It was a small place."

She recalls it cluttered with baseball bats, basketballs and hockey sticks.

"He played all sorts of sports," Martin said.

It was baseball that made Fergie famous. The tall right-handed pitcher, who for the past 13 years has been living and working on his own ranch in Oklahoma, retired with 267 complete games and 49 shutouts. He was a 20-game winner seven times, with six of those in consecutive years.

Fergie also holds the ninth-highest strikeout total in history (3,192) and was the National League Cy Young Award winner in 1971. In 1991, he was inducted into Cooperstown's Baseball Hall of Fame.

Martin said the home could serve a number of purposes, one being as part of the continuing cultural history of blacks in Canada that begins with the Underground Railway.

"In fact, it could be part of the tour of the Underground Railway," she said.

Contacted in Chatham, where he was autographing copies *The Game Is Easy, Life Is Hard*, a biography of him written by Dorothy Turcotte, Jenkins said, "I'm delighted to hear someone wants to open a museum, but I didn't know the house was for sale.

"I spent 16 years of my life in that place. I threw balls in the front yard and on the street."

Stories abound about Fergie's youth. Gene Dziadura, who had been with the Phillies organization as a scout, told Fergie he'd never pitch in the big leagues till he built up some upper body strength. He ordered Fergie to chop wood all winter before he'd take a look at him.

Dziadura finally got the young Fergie hurling balls on winter nights and weekends in the gym at Chatham Collegiate Institute.

The other thing the aspiring ball player did to build up his strength was to take a five-pound sledgehammer and pound it into a pillow with his right hand. He'd raise the hammer slowly by the end of the handle, then let it slam down into a pillow on the kitchen table. It drove his mother crazy, but she put up with it, like so many other things. Like the time Fergie was nearly blinded when he had gone down by the river to have a marshmallow roast with his buddies.

At one point while leaning over to blow out a flaming marshmallow, one of the friends shoved Fergie and the burning stick landed in his face, causing third degree burns to his eyelids, cheeks and eyebrows. His mother was beside herself. She knew how close he'd come to losing his sight. She lost her sight from complications during 14 hours of labour on Dec. 13, 1943, giving birth to Fergie.

The house on Adelaide is where Fergie spent most of his childhood and adolescence. That's why it delights him to know that someone might consider turning the place into a museum.

He's promised to provide valuable memorabilia he's kept all these years from his life in baseball.

It'll be a homecoming he'll look forward to. [Aug. 13, 2002]

Fighter With Inside Connections To Main Event

[Les Temesy]

HE LOOKS LIKE A FIGHTER. There's a roughness to his voice. And when he talks about the old days of battling in the gyms in Detroit in the 1940s, he's up on his feet, dancing about the living room, fists assaulting the air.

"I'm not telling you my age—everyone here wants to know my age! I'm old!"

This is Les Temesy, a fellow raised in gyms in Windsor and Chatham. A fellow who barnstormed Kent County fall fairs beating up on big strapping farmers who challenged him. A fellow who sparred with Jake LaMotta weeks before the Bronx Bull stole the middleweight title from Marcel Cerdan in 1949. A fellow who sparred with Rocky Graziano and Sugar Ray Robinson.

As you scan the pictures on the walls of his house, other names emerge from his past. What's Ralph Capone, Al's younger brother, doing here? Or Sol Goldman, the burlesque show millionaire who had close associations with Detroit's infamous Purple Gang?

Temesy chummed with these fellows, mostly through his close association with Goldman, who put up money for him to open up a clothing store in Amherstburg.

"He was like a father to me!" He then explains how Goldman used to lend money to the Purples, before fleeing Detroit to settle here.

The distance wasn't great enough to separate Goldman from mob figures who often made their way to meet him at his Blue Haven Motel at the edge of town.

Temesy recalls syndicate boss Pete Licavoli trying to strong-arm Goldman into some arrangement. His bodyguard actually had his hands around Goldman's neck and was roughing him up when Temesy rushed in from the other room with a fireplace poker and whacked this henchman across the ear, splitting it wide open. A scuffle ensued, but Temesy slammed a door on the bodyguard.

Don't misunderstand. Temesy kept his nose clean. For years, he operated a boxing club in Amherstburg out of the old town hall. He trained Windsor's Charlie Stewart, and Nino Valdes, the Cuban heavyweight champion who fought Sonny Liston and Archie Moore.

The times Temesy casts his mind back to are those formative years in Detroit when he turned pro. He won his Golden Gloves there, but the big money lured him. Joe Bomerito, a flamboyant nightclub owner with ties to the mafia, took him under his wing as manager. "I only found out later about his connections . . . All I knew was he had this big Lincoln and owned some nightclubs."

Temesy himself had 16 professional fights. Lost his first two, knocked out seven. "I just didn't have the killer instinct—I was having too much fun."

Those were heady days. Fighters streamed in from Chicago to train in Detroit. The mafia swarmed around. So did the women. "These guys (fighters) all had great looking broads!" Temesy said, remarking how LaMotta's Vicki—later featured in Playboy—was a real looker. He remembers her at the Book Cadillac after LaMotta's beating of Cerdan, and how the underworld goons crowded the hallways outside their room.

Temesy had sparred with LaMotta weeks in advance of that June 16, 1949 bout at Brigg's, later called Tiger, Stadium.

"Jake was like a freak—an oversized hand and spindly legs like Babe Ruth . . . He had a few screws loose. All those guys did."

Temesy sat in the front row, near LaMotta's corner, at that fight. In the second round, he spotted how Cerdan had been hurt when LaMotta threw him to the mat. Temesy leaned over and whispered to the fighter's manager, "Marcel (Cerdan) can't lift his right arm."

At the end of the round, the manager rushed to the corner to tell Jake, and from that point on, Jake worked that arm and finally won the fight after 10 rounds.

There in those Detroit gyms downtown, Temesy got to know fighters like LaMotta, but also Graziano and Sugar Ray. Of Sugar Ray, he remembered, "It was embarrassing to be in the same ring with him—he was so good . . . He could knock you out with either hand!"

The pictures on the wall speak for themselves.

So do the 16-ounce boxing gloves hanging limply from a nail. He had used those mitts to battle LaMotta in the sweaty gym off Woodward in Detroit 52 years ago. [Feb. 22, 2002]

Hard As Nails

[Raymond "Mickey" Warner]

IF YOU LIVE IN THE EAST END OF THE CITY, you might see him running. Five miles a day along the Ganatchio Trail.

Raymond "Mickey" Warner is now 72, but old habits die hard. From about the age of 14, he gravitated to the boxing ring. And he's managed to keep in shape ever since. Running. And running. The mainstay of a boxer.

It's the first piece of advice he gives when I ask him what's the secret to training.

"Running!" he shoots back.

And skipping and finding "natural balance."

I ask Mickey what he means by that, and there's no hesitation as he recounts how in the old days when every spare moment was spent in the gym training boxers, he'd pull a young boxer aside and order them "to walk." He said, "I'd watch the way they walked, and tell them to look in the mirror, and that's the way I wanted them to stand when they were in the ring.

"As natural as the way they walked."

The other day when Mickey was studying the movement of some fighters in the ring, he noticed many stood with their feet "too far apart." He said, "They can't move when their feet are so far apart."

Mickey Warner is still a household name in this city. Some remember him as the feisty former president of Local 82 of the Canadian Union of Public Employees, whose clashes with the city are legendary. Others know him as the chief negotiator for the Canadian Bridge Unit of the United Steelworkers of America. Others see him as that scrappy fighter from the west end who, at 21, became Canada's featherweight champion and the Michigan Golden Gloves champion.

Much later, Mickey was training boxers in the basement of Holy Rosary Church on Drouillard, and later across from Windsor Arena in the old gas company building. It was in those gyms that he took Johnny Kubinec, Stan Renaud, Phil Parent and others under his tutelage and led them to win the Golden Gloves in Michigan in 1958.

He carries a picture of those fighters with him, an old black and white photograph. It gives him so much pride. I look at this man holding that photograph, and I see someone with the pug nose and battered ears, and think here's someone who looks like a fighter. The stereotype. But behind the tough guy veneer—and there was nobody tougher at the bargaining tables—there's that sentimental soul that still pines for the old days.

But really, is that what it is all about? I think it has more to do with perfection and seeing these boxers hone their skills, working day and night, pushing themselves beyond all their dreams and then finally seeing them dance in the ring with their arms raised high in victory.

Mickey—too slight for football and too short for basketball—learned the hard way. It's been said he battled in the streets before taking to the ring.

A memory Mickey still nurtures is from the early 1960s in Chicago when he noticed a lanky kid with long arms and lightning speed battering his opponents with ease. Mickey was there with his own team but was asked to help out "in the corner" for this black boxer.

"I wasn't doing anything special—just giving him water and that sort of thing."

Then he saw the fighter move into the ring, and marvelled at his grace.

Years later, he watched this same fighter take on the Heavyweight Champion of the World—Sonny Liston. And he saw Liston go down to defeat.

That fighter, whose corner he had worked, was Cassius Clay, later called Muhammad Ali. [Sept. 17, 2004]

16th Round Draft Pick

[Dave Liffiton]

TWO MINUTES INTO THE GAME he went over the boards and for the first time in his life was skating his dream.

The National Hockey League. Skating his heart out under the gorgeous glare of Madison Square Gardens. It wasn't the same as playing in Hartford. It wasn't the same as playing anywhere. It was a blur of colour and faces, his heart was pounding, and there wasn't a thought in his brain.

Except to keep his feet moving.

Before he knew it, he had a penalty. A tripping penalty. And if there was any consolation to it, he was in the record books.

His first game in the NHL. His first penalty.

I'm talking about Dave Liffiton, a 21-year old who grew up in Windsor playing house league and finally AAA hockey. The year he was drafted—16th round by the Plymouth Whalers in 2000—there wasn't a team in these parts that would take him. Not Tecumseh. Not Leamington. Not Chatham.

And so the kid went "down the road," as he says, to Aylmer, and played there. The following season, he had cracked the lineup in Plymouth. In June 2003, Dave was a second-round draft pick by the NHL's Colorado Avalanche. Since then, he's been involved in a trade that sent him to the Big Apple to join the Rangers. With that, Dave was dispatched to one of its affiliates, first in Charlotte, N.C., then to New York's AHL team in Hartford, only two hours down the road from Madison Square Gardens.

He's done well there, but there was no way he was thinking he'd get a call to play his first game in the NHL.

"It really caught me off guard," he said.

That call, however, came last week during practice. His coach summoned him from the ice, and told him to pack his bags, that he would be in the lineup with the Rangers that night. The next few hours went by in a flash. As Dave packed up in the locker room, he coaxed the trainer to fetch pasta from a place across the street from the arena.

"So when I got home, I was rushing around, eating and packing," Dave said.

Then he was on the road.

That night, he wore number 55 with his name emblazoned on the back.

"I was nervous, everything was so fast. It was like a blur out there."

After taking the penalty, it made his next shift even worse, because he didn't want to screw up.

"I realized then what they (the coaches) had told me before the game—just keep playing the way you do in Hartford. I concentrated on that, and I started settling down."

Seventeen shifts later, and a 3-2 loss to the New York Islanders, Dave's first game was over, and he was heading back to Hartford, but with the hope of returning for the playoffs.

That would be special.

That would be special, not just for the experience, but also for another reason. That reason has its roots in the stories that ignited Dave's imagination as a boy. He grew up hearing tales of his great-grandfather, Ernie Liffiton Sr., who played for the Stanley Cup winning Montreal Wanderers in 1907 alongside Art Ross.

"His name is on the cup," said Dave.

It was his grandfather that sat the young Liffiton down and conjured those early days when Ernie, Sr. played with Cyclone Taylor and Lester and Frank Patrick. And the other night when Dave had finished playing his first game in the NHL, he got to thinking about something his grandfather had told him.

"It was one of the last things he told me . . . And it started to sink in, I guess.

"The last time I saw him was when I had gone back home (to Windsor) around Halloween, and my grandfather had cancer, and didn't have long . . . As a matter of fact, he died in November.

"I remember the last thing he told me. He said, 'Keep working hard . . . I know you'll make it . . . You'll have to get the Liffiton name on that cup again." [April 19, 2006]

Float Like A Butterfly, Fall Like A Lead Balloon

[Border City Boxing Club]

MUHAMMAD ALI TOLD ME YEARS AGO IN AN INTERVIEW how he wore down the monster George Foreman and beat him with one good punch. The Canadian writer Morley Callaghan spoke to me about how he KO'd Ernest Hemingway in a boxing ring in Paris in the 1920s. And I was ringside when Felix Savon, the legendary Cuban heavyweight, knocked out a Puerto Rican boxer at the PanAm Games in Argentina with two punches in the first 20 seconds of the first round.

As a boy of eight, my older brothers shoved me into a makeshift boxing ring in the basement of our house in old Riverside and stood back and watched me take a beating from all the older kids in the neighbourhood.

That was 1954. Now 50 years later, I am standing at centre ring at the Border City Boxing Club on Drouillard Road. Hands taped. Sixteen-ounce gloves. Headgear. Mouthpiece. Lloyd Johnson, my corner guy, has greased up my face.

I'm here to get a taste of what it means to be in the ring. Something I had always dreamed of. My mantra is: "Float like a butterfly, sting like a bee."

But there's no dance in my feet. They feel like lead. And I can't see. Someone nearby has pocketed my tri-focals and the room is swimming in a blur. And Josh "Jackknife" Cameron, my opponent—a two-time Ontario champ—is an apparition. I watch him dance, his head bobbing up and down like a swimmer in a summer lake. I figure I should wait him out, and get him to make the first move.

Boom, boom! The first punch, and he's hit me dead on in the face. Boom, boom! Jackknife's done it again before I can figure out just how he managed that with my dukes up. I better retaliate, but my swing goes wild, and I slice the air like a blind man. Josh Canty, Border City Boxing Club owner, is screaming for me to throw my right. I do. But can't touch this guy. Boom! And Jackknife slams me with a body shot. I'm beginning to believe there's got to be more than one fighter out there because I'm getting nailed from all sides.

Boom! A shot to the side of the head. Where the hell did that come from?

Boom! Boom!

Keep low, I think. Keep low. Keep moving. Forget the mantra.

Despite the blurred vision, I can see this guy is smiling. Maybe laughing at me. I'm a target. And this is target practice for him. I know I must change the momentum. Jackknife's beating me on points. I'll rush him, and I do. But I stumble as I drive him to the ropes, and he nearly trips, mostly because I'm stepping on his right foot. My heart is pumping with the thought I might knock him down from sheer clumsiness. But Jackknife recovers quickly, and I sustain a barrage of shots—first to the ribs, then to the head, then to the shoulder, then to the head. Holy mackerel! How many arms does he have? I'm running out of gas. I'm praying for the bell. This is the longest two minutes of my life.

Boom! Boom! My lungs are burning.

I take another rush at Jackknife, and completely lose sight of him. Where the hell did he go? Is this blind man's bluff? Pin the tail on the donkey? Boom! Another body shot. A sharp reminder he's still in the ring.

"Nice move, Marty!" I hear from the corner. Is that sarcasm?

The bell.

My lungs are going to explode. I lean on the ropes. My heart is jumping in my chest like a muskie. I spit out the mouthpiece. But I'm back for the second round. I can barely lift my arms. I'm done but I shuffle forward like a feeble octogenarian, and know Jackknife is moving in for the kill. He's still smiling.

My pathetic debut as a boxer.

Boom! Boom! Boom!

The next thing I know I'm kneeling in the ring. I figure he can't hit me if I'm kneeling. I'm finished. Then I see the towel floating over my head and alighting like a beautiful morning dove on the canvas. It's over.

Thank you, Lord!

P.S. Jackknife is 14 years old—43 years younger than I am, if that's a significant detail for this story. [April 1, 2004]

Tale Of A Legend

[Joe Louis]

HE REACHED DOWN AND TIGHTENED THE LACES ON HIS BOOTS. He looked out across the open stretch of farm fields near Stoney Point. Then started trotting.

His breath was visible in the cold winter air. The wind from the lake pushed at his back. Running. Kicking up the dusty white snow on the roads.

For all of his mighty stature in the boxing ring, his hulking figure now on this windy road in December 1950 was dwarfed by the flat-as-a-table landscape. Running. Running. Three miles in the cold. Beside him, a trainer. Yet the big man seemed alone. Alone with his thoughts, probably fixed on the fight ahead, the taste of victory or perhaps defeat, maybe the money purse, the bad investments, the huge expectations. The risk of getting hurt.

Already Joe Louis was a legend.

That weighed upon him. The fight with Ezzard Charles that past September was something he needed to shake. The press said he was washed up, overweight, no longer the giant of the ring. He had lost to Charles in a 15-round slugfest at New York's Yankee Stadium. Knew he could've done better. Knew he was better than the papers said. Now, three months later, a few weeks before Christmas, he was trying to change things, to save face, to shake loose those who opposed him. Including creditors. Trying to get back his old form. To tell the world he was still a champion.

All Joe Louis wanted was to be back in the mix, under an arena's hot lights, to drink in the din of the crowds. He yearned for it. It was said he'd breathe a sigh of relief every time the door to his dressing room opened, and he stepped out into the arena. He felt back at home, among his kind, the master of his fate.

That winter of 1950, Joe Louis had chosen to train at Stoney Point, a tiny French-Canadian village, away from the bustle of Detroit. It was here he hoped to recapture the driving spirit that had made him mighty in the ring.

Louis and twenty close friends had opened the St. Clair Shores

Surf Club Resort. He had decided to use it now in the off-season with less than a month before he would meet Freddy Beshore at the Detroit Olympia.

The farm country of Stoney Point was abuzz. They'd spot the man they knew from the fights on the radio. There he was now, running the road, heading out along the Rochester Town Line. Or he might be spotted at Chez Cormier, a grocery store in Stoney Point where he ran a tab. He'd pile into a big Caddy and wend his way back home along the ditch-lined roads.

It was said he once hitched a ride on a tractor with a farmer. The former heavyweight, called "The Brown Bomber," was chauffeured back to his waterfront estate. He promised to leave the farmer a pair of tickets at the Olympia.

Louis worked hard at Stoney Point. And when he'd stepped into the ring Jan. 3, 1951 at the Olympia, Louis had trimmed down to 212 pounds, his lowest fight weight since beating Joe Walcott in 1947.

At the makeshift ring at St. Clair Shores, he sent many a sparring partner home, hurting. The Brown Bomber felt healthy. Boasted to the press of never being "hurt." All Charles had given him was a black eye. Nothing more.

That Jan. 3, under the lights of the Olympia, Louis was his old self, crushing Beshore in the fourth round with blow after blow until the referee ruled it finished.

Back on track. Louis thanked Stoney Point. A swaggering confidence in his comeback, ready to take on the rising star, the young Rocky Marciano. Eight months later, Louis fell in the eighth round. Tired legs. A broken heart.

After the fight, Joe lay on the rubbing table—his right ear cushioned by a towel, a raincoat draped over him, left hand stuck in an ice bucket. The reporters forced to kneel at his side with their heads close to his lips just to hear him.

A sad ending for the great man.

Back in Stoney Point, the owners of Chez Cormier wondered if he'd ever be back to settle his account. [Sept. 30, 2002]

Former Tiger Still Enjoying The Game Of Life

[Reno Bertoia]

HE GLIDES WITH THE PUCK, hoping for a teammate to make a break to the left. And when it happens, he swiftly passes the black disc to a forward. He does this with a smoothness reminiscent of a ballplayer who once made a double play look as easy as setting down a cup on a kitchen table.

Reno Bertoia is back in uniform.

Wearing number 16. Same number he wore with the Detroit Tigers in the '50s and '60s at the corner of Michigan and Trumbull.

This time, Reno's on the ice.

On skates. Tuesday and Friday mornings. His 63-year-old heart pounding in his chest. Playing with the Bendo Blazers.

Two teams. The white shirts and blue shirts.

Reno suits up with the blues.

Life has come full circle for the former infielder who led the American League in hitting for about a month and a half one summer in the 1950s, shaming the great Ted Williams.

Before breaking into the big leagues in 1953, Bertoia played "the sandlots." He batted .380 with the Detroit Amateur Baseball Federation and represented Michigan in the National All Star game in New York.

"I was having fun with baseball then, but when I got into the majors, it wasn't fun anymore. . . . It got to be a job.

"Now with hockey, I'm having fun again."

The Italian-born Bertoia, who came to Canada when he was two, grew up in the Hickory Road area. He played ball in an empty field next to the old incinerator plant, then later at Stodgell Park. In those days, kids batted around taped baseballs and scrounged gloves from neighbours.

"I never owned a glove until I signed pro," says Bertoia smiling about how he borrowed gloves from Hank Biasetti, a former Philadelphia Athletics ballplayer who lived nearby. "He'd bring home a glove every season and give it to me."

In those days, playing ball was Bertoia's life. He dreamed of the big leagues. Couldn't wait to jump out of bed in the morning and round up the guys, and play until dusk.

As Bertoia got into organized ball, he was like a panther in the field, snagging errant balls, keeping his team in the game. That's how he got noticed. How people came to believe in him.

"I worked under the tutelage of Father (Ronald) Cullen (at Assumption) who brought out the potential I had."

Bertoia was lucky. He jumped right into the majors. He can't forget that September day at Tiger Stadium in 1953. His first time at bat. Against the legendary Satchel Paige.

"I was scared to death . . . I saw three pitches . . . And it was 'See you later.'"

Reno had come into the majors with Al Kaline, and roomed with him all those years with the Tigers. But when the team was in town, Reno stayed at home, sleeping in his boyhood room on Langlois Avenue where his parents had moved. Afternoons after a game, Reno would bring some of the players home, where his mother had steaming plates of pasta waiting. Sitting around the table would be Billy Martin, Ray Boone, Al Aber and Ned Garver. The neighbourhood was abuzz with these major leaguers stopping in for dinner. And kids swarmed the Bertoia home.

Those were good times.

Reno was at home. Playing and living the good life. But always hitting the books. Trying to get good marks at Assumption.

"One day I wrote an exam, and later that day had to face (Hall of Famer) Early Wynn . . . I didn't do well with either one."

Bertoia played from 1953 to 1958 with the Tigers before going to the Washington Senators. His playing career ended with the Hanshin Tigers in Japan. In Japan he was made to feel like somebody. He was recognized on the streets and in clubs. He had a good time there.

"I saw something in baseball that I'd never seen before, and that was in a game where the manager of the other team walked out to the mound, and instead of calling a pitcher from the bullpen, he called in a new catcher."

Reno's last game in baseball was in Hiroshima.

After baseball, Bertoia taught high school, retiring from

Assumption. He also did some scouting for the Tigers and wears a 1968 World Series ring. Not as a player, but as a scout.

In 1995 he was diagnosed with prostate cancer and had surgery to remove it. Touch wood, he says, he's fine. It was a life being given back to him. That makes this special. The circling about the ice. The sport of just *being*.

Reno scored his first goal a few months ago.

"The guys gave me the puck . . . It's in my bag."

He smiles.

The puck likely won't make it to the collection of baseballs—the homerun ball, his first in the majors—that sits on display in his living room.

Then again . . . [Feb. 20, 1998]

OHL Draft

[Steph Gervais]

THE DARKNESS LIFTS ON THIS JUNE MORNING. Not quite 5:30. We're barreling down a smooth, open stretch of highway to Toronto. I'm thinking, this is appropriate isn't it? On the road at dawn. For years I've chauffeured my kids to hockey rinks. Tied up their skates, carried their bags, and sticks, and ran to the snack bar to get them drinks. And stood morning after morning, and weekend after weekend, in frigid arenas around town, my tongue stinging from that first sip of hot coffee. Bored, sleepy. Every now and again, ambling out to the car, turning it on and slumping back to half listen to the radio, and maybe fall asleep if I was lucky.

Then the drive home, struggling to be encouraging. Putting on a pot of oatmeal, and getting ready for work. I'm thinking, this is appropriate—I'm on my way to Brampton, to the OHL draft, and my kid, who once could sprawl on the backseat, and still have room, now—all six-foot-two of him—sits with his knees up around his face because it's so cramped in my car.

Also traveling with Steph is an uncle, and my oldest son, André, who, besides playing with the Essex 73s, flirted briefly with professional hockey in the Czech Republic, and with teams in Jacksonville, Fla., and Macon, Ga. He's secretly proud of his brother, even though two or three years ago he predicted there wasn't a chance in hell of his snotty-faced sibling ever playing serious hockey.

This runs through my mind as the two try to sleep in the car.

All those weekends when my friends were running off to concerts or dinner parties, I was on the road, sleeping in motel rooms reeking of sweaty hockey gear. And privately cursing fatherhood.

Here I am, on the road again.

This isn't the story of first round draft picks. This isn't the story of potential superstars. This is a Canadian story. An ordinary kid, only 16, riding that long ribbon of highway to Brampton with hopes and dreams. Just like any other kid. Knowing he could just as easily face disappointment. That's OK. That's part of the process. For any kid. Success and failure.

Being benched, being hailed, being yelled at, being praised.

They know disappointment.

They've played on losing teams.

They've missed a perfect shot.

They've made a bad pass that landed up on someone else's stick and the other team ended up scoring and winning the game.

They've stared disappointment in the face. They're ready for it.

So here we are. Arriving in Brampton. After a few moments, the legendary Bobby Orr shows up with families of various draft picks he's promoting. They literally take over the section we're sitting in. All of these kids go in the first few rounds.

Morning turns to late afternoon. We're now all alone in what once seemed a lucky section. My oldest boy is slumped over two or three seats, bored out of his mind.

"I think the luck here has run out," Steph says, realizing now this isn't going his way. Still, he's happy to be there. And cheers Essex 73s teammate, Shane Tatomir for going to the Spitfires. Also smiles genuinely for buddies, Mike James and Bryan Dennison.

Steph silently watches grinning families mill about the vast arena floor as kids pull on team jerseys and get pictures taken. Perhaps feels like a player on the third line who may never see the action. Yet content to be there, to be part of the process. And that's enough.

By the 14th round, he's certain it's not going to happen. Yet, still no sign of defeat in his eyes. Disappointment seemingly not a part of his vocabulary. Then suddenly Steph looks up from the OHL program notes to hear his name over the din of the arena—the Plymouth Whalers are drafting him.

His mind is a whirl as he walks like a somnambulist to the floor. They're handing him a jersey. Putting it over his head. I stand beside his towering height like a golly gee kid brother.

This is what it's all about.

A kid, any kid, no better than anybody else, but someone who works hard, and maybe is good enough to get this far, and maybe no further.

But he knows that. Knows too it's OK to taste this single, pure moment of success. No matter how fleeting. [June 9, 1999]

Rink Rat

[Frank Matthy]

FRANK MATTHYS DOESN'T LIVE FAR FROM THE ARENA. He knows it like the back of his hand. He's 79 and can't forget the day when those now-crumbling walls went up around what had been a modest outdoor rink. He also can't forget the taste of victory—that sweetness when his beloved Essex '73s Junior C club galloped to victory in what might well be the coldest arena in southwestern Ontario.

"Home," is the way Frank describes the old place that has virtually been his refuge from the world and where he's hung his hat for nearly 35 years. Frank was there last week knocking on the doors of this 45-year-old building, and asking about its future.

But the padlocks have been on the arena for a week, though with any luck, they'll be off, or at least Frank hopes they will, so he can return to his '73s.

This grizzly-looking man is really the soul behind the team. And maybe the one person who knows this old building better than anybody. He doesn't need a blueprint or a map. He knows every square inch and cubbyhole. And when it comes to the game of hockey, Frank's the one fellow all the players go to. The one who quietly bolsters the moody top scorers who grind away in a slump. The one who soothes the down-in-the-dumps attitude of rookies toiling on a fourth line.

Frank's not a coach, not a general manager and he hasn't a penny invested in this team. In truth, he's the one who makes sure the water bottles are filled, the dressing rooms cleaned and uniforms washed. A thankless job, but Frank goes about it with a smile.

His desire is to be behind the bench, to pat a player on the back when they slide back to the bench after a good shift, or to perk them up. And it's not strategy for the ice that he doles out to these boys—it's life lessons.

Being positive.

That's the way Frank is today about the old barn.

I've known him for a number of years. And thought of him the other day when I read about the difficulties and the unsettling future

95

of the 45-year-old Essex Arena. I know there are plans to rebuild it, and a proposal to go ahead with a $7-million expansion and a new ice pad.

But at the moment, the priority is to do something about the cracking walls at the northeast corner and make repairs to five of eleven arches that support the building.

Frank, who is never without a ball cap, is an optimist and someone who loves the old place, its character and feel. Loves it like an old dog that he won't get rid of. For him, it's an old-time Ontario arena: A bit rundown at the heels and all, and a place with that unmistakable commingling of odours from wretched hockey bags and popcorn and french fries.

It's home.

It's about tradition. It's where the Crowders made history. It's where boys from all over the area have come with dreams of one day skating on the big ice surfaces with the hockey greats. It's where it's not uncommon to find someone at the upper rail reaching into an inside coat pocket for a flask, pouring a bit of hard stuff into a Styrofoam cup of coffee to keep warm. It's where fans come with blankets to wrap around themselves. It's where the smokers congregate outside the entrance even on the coldest nights of the year. It's where the sharp-eyed scouts have elbowed their way into a position behind the glass with their clipboards in search of future stars.

Frank has seen it all.

"I'm the original," he once told me.

The real McCoy.

The original and consummate rink rat, who started as a goal judge some 30 years ago. Another thankless job that one night got Frank into big trouble when an irate fan didn't like his call and came at him with fire in his eyes. He was swift to wrestle this man to the floor and hold him down till he got help.

The stories are endless about the old place.

So are the dreams.

Keep them alive. [Dec. 2, 2005]

Wildcats

[Janna Desmarais]

SHE GRINNED FROM EAR TO EAR as she made those first strides out on the smooth gleaming surface of the ice. But suddenly her smiling turned to a frown as Janna Desmarais glanced down at her skates for half a second. It was as if she was gently coaxing her feet to remember what it was like to be on skates, and to be back on the ice again.

It seemed so long ago.

It was seven months almost to the day when she last laced up those skates for the Windsor Wildcats and scored a goal in a 6-0 win in Rochester, New York. But all the glory of that moment in January is marred by the nightmare that unfolded only a few hours later when the chartered team bus Janna was riding in veered off Interstate 390 and slammed into a parked tractor-trailer.

That January 29th accident claimed the lives of her coach, Rick Edwards, his 13-year-old son, Brian, and Cathy Roach, a hockey mom. Janna herself suffered two broken legs and a collapsed lung.

"We thought we had lost her," Tracy Desmarais, her mother, told me.

Thursday afternoon, with titanium rods and four screws still lodged in her scarred legs, Janna stepped out on the ice, determined to put that horror behind her. She was joined by teammates and friends for a light skate. Her hope is to get a jump on September's training camp.

"She's been dreaming of this moment," said her mother. "Even a few weeks after the accident, she was talking about getting back on the ice.

"It's been her passion, and I think it's what has kept her going . . . Doing the therapy and getting stronger, all so she can get back on the ice."

That day in January, however, is not easily forgotten: "There isn't a day that goes by that I don't think of it . . . It keeps running in my head.

"What I remember is sleeping (on the bus) then waking, and feeling something jolting . . . I thought I was still dreaming.

"I could hear the sound of metal crunching and glass breaking, and then everything was silent, so, so quiet.

"Then the screaming.

"At first I couldn't scream. I couldn't get anything out . . . Nothing.

"And I didn't feel any pain and that scared me . . . The seats in front had crushed my legs . . . I thought my legs were gone, and my first thought was, as funny as this might sound, 'I can't play hockey now.'"

The next thing Janna knew, she was being airlifted by helicopter and then she was lying in the emergency room at Strong Memorial Hospital in Rochester. From that point on, until February 11th when hospital staff moved her to another room, she has little recollection.

A few months ago, the team was invited to go for a ride on a bus, just around the parking lot in Essex.

"It was eerie because we sat in all the same spots we always did. And we'd look around at each other and say, 'I didn't realize you were that close to me.'

"That's the only time I've been on a bus since the accident."

Her eagerness and determination to play hockey have never wavered. Hobbling about the backyard, she's been shooting balls at a net, just to get a feel of the stick in her hands. And in May, Janna tried to yank on her skates, but her feet were still too swollen.

"I had to wait, but now I'm ready," she told me in the dressing room.

"I've been dying to get back, and I don't know whether I'm ready to play again. But it's what I want most."

And when she first stepped out on the ice, Janna could hear the pounding on the glass as family and friends applauded her return. Her aunt, Sue Caza, wiped away some tears as she watched her niece glide about the arena.

"We've all been waiting so long for this."

It wasn't long before Janna was back at the boards and resting on her hockey stick.

"So what's it like?" I asked.

"My ankles are killing me," she said with a smile. Then she rushed off again to skate with the puck.

I knew what she was feeling. She had spoken of it earlier. I knew as she made that first pass around the ice, she could hear the sound of the skates meeting the ice. And it was music to her ears, music to her heart.

It was worth the wait. [Aug. 25, 2005]

A Bad Leg and a Good Arm

[Don Gardiner]

IT WAS NEAR THE END OF THE THIRD PERIOD. I noticed him on a high stool behind the net. He had a set of crutches shoved under his seat. A tiny heater cranked away at his feet.

The man was Don Gardiner, goal judge for the Sarnia Junior B Steeplejack Bees.

A loquacious, congenial man.

We got talking. The game was 2-1 in favour of Leamington. Not much action at Don's end.

We talked about how tight a game it was, the fortunes of hockey and draft picks, the amenities of arenas, the politics of minor hockey, the All Star game, the weather, kids in sports, and finally baseball.

"You know my son used to play for Sparky."

His son is Mike Gardiner, a relief pitcher for the Detroit Tigers from 1993 to 1995. He also played for Montreal, Seattle and Boston.

I remembered Gardiner in Detroit. A big six-foot right-hander. Actually saw him pitch in spring training in Lakeland, Fla.

"You know, when he was in Montreal, they told him they had 15 different signs for a bunt. When he came to Detroit, Mike went to Billy Muffett and asked about the signs, and Muffett kinda looked at him as if to say, 'What do you mean?' And Mike told him about Montreal and Muffett made it sound so simple. He told him, 'Look if it's a bunt, you make the play, pick up the ball and throw it to first . . .'"

Nothing complicated.

Another story: Mike faced Jose Canseco and had gone to a full count.

"He threw him a curve and Canseco just stood there and it curved over the plate for the strike.

"He didn't raise his bat . . . he was out and he just stood there and glared at Mike."

In the last inning of that same game, with two out . . . Mike had again gone to a full count against Canseco.

"Do you know what Mike threw?"

Before I could answer, Don said, "A backdoor curve."

"And got him?"

Without averting his eyes from the game, Don just nodded and smiled.

A proud father.

A hockey goal judge wearing a Sarnia Steeplejack jacket and talking about his boy in baseball.

A son who played seven years in the majors and now works as a day trader in Charlotte, N.C.

Don mused about those childhood years, coaching his son. Hot summer days. His boy then behind the plate, barely a teen and catching strikes. Dreaming of making it in baseball.

For Don, it was the love of the game that kept him in it. He yearned for those first moments in the spring, with its uncertain skies, and the cold reaching into the bones.

The thrill of it all. The excitement of getting back on the diamond, hearing the familiar crack of a bat and watching the ball sail in the open air.

Now 68, Don, a retired salesman, sits behind the glass and behind the net, ready to flip the switch and turn the lights red with a goal.

But nothing's happening.

Don tells me how Mike turned from catching to pitching at 17. He had filled in for someone in a game and proved to be a formidable hurler.

I asked Don about the crutches and he told me it's because polio has caught up with him again. As a boy, this same disease prevented him from playing baseball and hockey. But he loved both games. Loved the action.

When he was healthier, he was drawn back into sports—coaching baseball in Courtright where Mike first played and eventually, managing Mooretown's Junior C club.

Fifteen years ago, Don turned to goal judging. It's kept him busy. Now, he sits with the heater buzzing and his eye trained on the ice. He can tell you a story about each of the boys out there. Probably knows them like his own. Knows their dreams. And knows, too, if there's enough desire, anything's possible. [Feb. 7, 2001]

Fight Night at the Old Barn

[Jeff Kugel]

HIS SIX-FOOT-SEVEN, 255-POUND FRAME DWARFS HIS BEDROOM. Size 16 shoes—as large as twin skate boards—rest in front of the clothes closet. He slumps on the bed.

On the wall in front of him is a Wal-Mart framed photograph of a pair of skates. The aphorism below reads: "It takes courage to have a dream and determination to make it come true."

Eighteen-year-old Jeff Kugel—facing a lifetime suspension from the OHL for an altercation at Windsor Arena last weekend—ponders the reality of that dream. A dream all boys nurture when they start out—wobbly and awkward and naïve on a pair of stiff skates in a cold arena—that someday he'll make it to the NHL.

"That's where I want to be," says Jeff. And he still clutches to that far-flung hope of a fat contract and buying a Harley, "the same as Bob Probert's." He's tucked a snapshot of that bike behind the framed picture.

Hanging from another corner of that same photograph is a pendant from a minor hockey tournament in Kitchener three years ago, and how he won it for the team with a goal in overtime.

Now, suddenly the big hulking "power forward," as Jeff likes to regard himself, wonders what went wrong. One punch and it's all over for him. One silly sucker punch and a career comes to a bewildering halt.

In his eyes that night, there was no fear. Fear of nobody, and no thing. Least of all his future in hockey. And he galloped about the ice in a victory dance, thinking the worst he would face might be missing a few games.

Now he faces a lifetime ban. At the doorstep of the NHL. He reads about himself, hears what's being said, spots his name in *Sports Illustrated*. The monster. Boris Karloff on skates. The goon. A pumped up player who can't skate worth a damn, the big dumb enforcer.

He's heard it all before. Ever since he was eight when he towered over his teammates, Jeff's size plagued him, stole that innocent boyish

102

joy out of growing up. He'd roll in bed at night, and wonder what was wrong with him.

Playing was never easy.

Unlike others his age, it meant enduring the catcalls from angry parents who—horrified at his size—would yell down from the stands at him, "Get him out of here. Get off the ice!" It's meant putting up with coaches from opposing minor hockey travel teams who knocked at his dressing room door, demanding to examine his birth certificate. "I was always bigger than anybody else, so it was hard to get the puck away from me," Jeff tells me, sitting now at the kitchen table, his head down, as he picks away at a bowl of rice.

It's here in this modest suburban home in Roseville, Mi., about 50 km east of Detroit, that he grew up, and fired pucks on the driveway. "It bothered me, what they used to say." As I look at Jeff Kugel—portrayed as "the monster," the wild-eyed man with hands the size of coal shovels—I see a boyish confusion swarming over his face. It speaks loudly of what he's going through.

"I've heard it all before—I'm tired of it. I hate talking about it." Yet he does. Knows he must. His four-year-old brother Derek sidles up, and Jeff Kugel's large arms, like kindly tree limbs, surround the boy. He gently kisses the top of his brother's head. A gentleness that belies the maniacal dance this young man did on the ice after downing Owen Sound player Juri Golicic and then chasing Chris Minard who fled like a scared jack rabbit.

Who is he? The Gentle Giant? The deadly Enforcer? Good or Evil? Jeff Kugel is a study in contrasts. A young man whose trade in hockey are his fists. Yet, the same kid was handed a Most Sportsman-Like Award in minor hockey. A kid who rarely got into fights, was never suspended, never thrown out of a game.

Yet legendary boxer Tommy Hearns pulled him aside one day at the Kronk Gym, where Jeff works out regularly, shadow boxing and sparring, and told him to quit hockey, and go into the ring.

"I just want to play hockey—that's all."

And so when he came into training camp two years ago for the Spits, he knew his future depended upon getting the attention of coaches. "I got into five fights." Former Spitfire D. J. Smith coached him. It was deliberate. It's what the team expected. And he delivered.

Now, it's what the fans grovel for, and that's why the old barn erupts every time Jeff steps on the ice. It's infectious, intoxicating, deafening. It can't help but fuel the adrenaline that gushes like gasoline in Jeff Kugel's blood.

"That's not the boy I coached," says 75-year-old John Keranen, who taught Kugel how to skate when he was eight years old. "He was a big kid, but always level-headed."

Jeff gets up from the table, slides the video cassette into the VCR, plays back the fight. Frame by frame. "I didn't lose it, you see" he says of his composure. The decision to fight was his.

His mother Kathleen that night spotted the coach shaking his head as her son mounted the boards to take off across the ice. The crowd was in a frenzy. "The rafters were shaking, and they were calling out his name—K-U-G-E-L! K-U-G-E-L!"

Kathleen, too, was caught up in the fury.

So was her son who romped across the ice like a warring hero. The place screaming in his ears. He felt good. He felt powerful. He felt on top of the world.

Yet claims he never lost control. Even in that wild ecstatic dance. It was just that. A whirling dance of victory. "Goal scorers can do it, why not me?

"And when Golicic went down, why didn't I jump all over him?"

"What were you thinking then?" I ask.

Jeff speaks about the thrill of the moment, the exhilaration, delivering the goods to his fans. No malice. No anger. Nothing. A little like the thrill he felt 10 years ago in his first hockey game. Scoring three goals. He was eight.

"I knew I wanted to play hockey then—I haven't given up."

The fighting? Part of the bigger picture.

It saddens Jeff that the road to the NHL has taken a legal detour. All his life, his size has got him into trouble. It used to be the parents screaming. Now it's the league officials. Worried about his potential danger. His lethal size. His mom has heard it all before.

"He's a good kid . . . He wouldn't hurt anybody. That's not him."

"But are you worried about him?" I persist.

"No, I worry about the others (whom he fights) . . .

"I also feel sad for him . . . The other day he said, 'Mom, maybe it's true—maybe I'm not meant to be there.'"

Though the doubts keep him awake at night, Jeff hasn't given up. In a small way, the hockey puck from the Hockey Hall of Fame sitting on his bedroom dresser symbolizes that all-consuming dream. A dream he won't set free.

"I want to play. I know that's where I'm the happiest." [Nov. 6, 1998]

Saints and Sinners

The Great Imposter

[Ferdinand Waldo Demara, Jr.]

HE WAS CALLED THE GREAT IMPOSTER. He was a shameless fake, a master of deceit. Universal Pictures made a movie of his life in 1960 that starred Tony Curtis. Scores of articles have been written about him.

But his greatest impersonation was of a surgeon from Grand Falls, N.B.

Ferdinand Waldo Demara, Jr. was a likeable fellow, who endeared himself to this family on the east coast, where he had been living with the Christian Brothers. At the time, he was impersonating a Christian Brother monk and was going by the name of "Brother John." He became good friends with Dr. Joseph Cyr. Demara had told the doctor he had been a physician before going into the religious life.

The two traded medical stories.

And Demara became a regular guest at Cyr's house. The doctor's wife, Lily, often put out an extra plate at dinnertime. Then suddenly Demara disappeared. The Cyrs figured he had been transferred to another religious community. But then Demara surfaced again. Or at least his name did. It hit the papers all across the country. This amiable religious brother had been exposed as a fake. He had swiped the medical credentials of his old friend, Dr. Cyr from Grand Falls, and was now performing surgery on the HMCS *Cayuga* in its support for American troops in the Korean War.

Demara had never been a surgeon, never even practised medicine, except for a brief stint as a hospital orderly. Otherwise, he had lived the life of an imposter. Posing as a psychologist, a prison warden who "reformed" one of our country's toughest cell blocks, a Doctor of Philosophy in applied psychology at a Pennsylvania college, a Trappist monk, a cancer researcher and policeman, to name but a few.

One claim also has him impersonating an engineer and working for Ford in Dearborn, Michigan.

Meanwhile, back in Grand Falls, Dr. Cyr and Lily in 1951 were reading about a doctor of the same name distinguishing himself as a surgeon in Korea. They didn't realize it was Demara, or Brother John, as they knew him.

But when Dr. Cyr—still shocked that his medical credentials had mysteriously vanished—contacted the RCMP, he learned someone was posing as a Canadian surgeon in Korea using his name. He quickly found out that Demara had swiped his medical diplomas.

"We never did get them back," 79-year-old Lily told me over the phone last week.

She confesses neither she nor her late husband felt "cheated."

Lily said, "I felt sorry for him—he was such a nice fellow. I had no reason not to believe he had been a doctor before, although he seemed very naive about medicine. I figured he hadn't practiced for a long time. Turns out he was a good actor."

Indeed.

Demara, who passed away in 1982, was American, not Canadian. He joined the Royal Canadian Navy in March 1951 after arriving at the recruiting office in Saint John, N.B., where he offered his professional services as a doctor.

Since medical officers were in short supply during the Korean War the navy didn't bother to check his background. Besides, Demara handed the navy his credentials—or Cyr's—and was immediately commissioned as a Surgeon-Lieutenant on the *Cayuga*, headed for Korean waters.

Despite never having studied medicine, Demara proved a brilliant student, possessing a photographic memory. Soon he was performing minor surgeries, including dental work on the *Cayuga*'s commander.

Demara's real test followed a commando-style raid off the west coast of Korea, where three South Korean guerrillas were seriously wounded. This imposter surgeon leapt to the challenge and removed a bullet from a man's chest, then discovered he also had a collapsed lung from tuberculosis. Six weeks later, the patient was jogging on the ship.

Bill Boudreau, who sailed with Demara, said it was a common feeling aboard the *Cayuga* that you'd never visit a doctor until you went ashore.

"You didn't trust them—but this fellow—Demara—we trusted."

According to Boudreau, Demara was amazing: "We would drop

him off in the jungle for a week at a time, and he'd drag the wounded out . . ."

His fellow officers were so impressed with Demara they recommended him for a medal. This ultimately exposed him.

The Canadian Government merely slapped him on the wrist, and Demara was off again, this time posing as a deputy sheriff in the U.S., where he was finally caught.

Boudreau remembers Demara as the one who raised the morale on the *Cayuga*: "It had been like poison on the ship until we went ashore to play baseball against some marines. Demara disappeared for a while during the game, and then we saw him returning in this truck loaded with beer. He knew how to make us feel good. After that, we never had a problem."

Long after Korea, in 1976, the real Dr. Cyr was on loan to Good Samaritan Hospital in Orange County, Calif. In the midst of surgery, he looked up, and spotted his old friend from Grand Falls, N.B.

It seems Demara had surfaced again—this time as the hospital's chaplain. [May 29, 2003]

She's The Queen Of Drouillard Road

[Margaret Sidoroff / Border City Boxing]

A SMALL BOY WITH THE HOOD UP OVER HIS HEAD walks hesitantly into her office. "Hey, how ya doin'?"

"Not bad," the boy mumbles.

Another boy standing behind him says, "Another fight and he's going to juvenile!"

To this, Margaret Sidoroff—fire in her eyes—leans forward in her chair, and says, "What did I tell you?" The boy mumbles again.

"What did I tell you about this?" And scolds him for fighting.

An odd thing, you might think, when the woman who's saying this holds three world-boxing titles. This is her gym. Border City Boxing. These are her kids. Kids from the street. The ones who showed up after she bought the place with Josh Canty, her trainer, and now husband. Kids who were hanging about outside. Nothing to do on a hot June day. So she said, "C'mon inside."

Once inside, Sidoroff laid down the rules: No swearing, no fighting with each other and you had better not get into any trouble on the streets. Otherwise you're out of here. No second chances.

There's a method to Sidoroff's madness. She's a counsellor at New Beginnings, an enclave for young offenders.

"I don't want them to end up there!"

To that end, she's yanked these kids off the street, put them to work in the gym, and there they skip rope, work the bag, shadow box, whatever she demands. And when they get home they're "too worn out" to do anything other than collapse on the couch and watch television.

Now that school's back, she's telling these kids they can't use the gym unless they've got their homework done. There are 23 kids. "They can't afford to pay me anything—I just take them in, an hour before everybody else, and I teach them a few things."

Sidoroff shrugs. There's no money in it and that may be bad business. But it's what she's all about. Her heart goes out to them. Like the little boy in the hooded sweatshirt. His father is a crackhead. His mother, just out of jail. "I teach these kids to respect each other. I teach them how to defend themselves without ever hitting anybody.

"And this little guy—the most polite little kid—I feel so sorry for him.

"He's always getting picked on because of his size. I tell him, 'You know you're a good kid. Always polite. Always good . . . But just keep your hands to yourself. Look, you can outrun anybody in this place and if someone throws a punch at you . . . sprint! Run!'"

Sidoroff knows all about this. Knows all about size. Five-foot-one, 110 pounds. Yet tough as nails. Enough that few fighters in the world want to do battle with her. But Sidoroff can talk her way through troubles. "I've always had a good sense of humour, I guess, and can talk my way out of anything."

It might be this she'll teach these kids—to do some talking, to lose the hard luck attitude, to find something to laugh about, and learn to walk away with pride, with confidence.

For Sidoroff, that's a battle she isn't willing to run from. It's on her turf, the boxing club. Here where the ring behind her looms like a dream with the glare of sun through the windows. Here where all around her are kids—some as young as 9 and 10—working the heavy bag, shadow boxing, skipping. They cry out to her from across the club—they seek approval.

"What do I do now?" one little guy yells.

"Hit the speed bag!" she shouts back.

A trace of a smile breaks on her face. She loves these kids. She sees in them hope. She sees a future for them. She sees the boxing ring teaching them discipline, self-control, hard work. It's worked for her. Two university degrees. A job as a counsellor. Three boxing titles. Hard work. Dedication. A love of life.

The 27-year-old fighter has landed on her feet here. She's the Queen of Drouillard. Toughest girl on the street. A big heart. Eager to please. Eager to change lives. [Sept. 20, 2000]

Breakfast With The Mayor

[David Burr]

AT THE BACK OF ELIAS DELI, a few men jostle to figure out who just walked in. "Hey, aren't you the former mayor?" Louie Sleiman, the gregarious, mustachioed cook, finally calls out.

The man, who sits down across from me at the table, smiles. "Yeah!" That same squeaky benign voice.

Louie turns to his friend, "I thought so! We looked at your picture up there! We thought that was you."

This man's picture was part of Louie's gallery of mayors, which dates back to the days of Art Reaume.

The smiling, grey-haired David Burr doesn't mind being noticed. It's been a long time since that's happened. Since his departure from politics that winter of 1988 after being mayor for three years, no one has called him, no one has bothered to stay in touch or to ask him what he thinks of changes in the city.

"I stopped looking at the paper, or the news on the television . . . I was out of the loop."

It seems, too, life has proven to be especially unkind to Windsor's former mayor. Today at 52, he lives in a mobile home in Lucier Estates in McGregor. On his own after two failed marriages and five troublesome years of unemployment. On his own, after being turned down for jobs all across the country.

The former chartered accountant and one-time mayor of this city now finds himself dealing blackjack three days a week at Casino Windsor. Some might see this as a fall from grace. David Burr disagrees: "This is not a come down—it's a comeback. I'm just happy to be working again."

And when Burr unzips his jacket, you see the bowtie, and checkered vest festooned with Casino buttons, his ID. He's identified as "David." No last name. "Occasionally someone at the casino tables will recognize me. They'll say, 'Don't I know you? Weren't you somebody once?'"

Maybe that's why he's surprised to see the picture in Louie's place. The hope in his eyes, the confidence. He hasn't tasted that for some time. Maybe that's why he gets up, and leans over the counter to get a better look at the framed picture.

It was taken on Election Night 1985—that triumphant pinnacle when he thumped his rival Al Santing by 10,000 votes and stole the city's top position.

Those were happier days. Better days. Top of the heap then. Full of ambition, vigor, vision. But things never seemed to click into place for David Burr. The worst was the nightmare over the proposed million dollar wave pool. The project—sharply ridiculed from all quarters—killed David Burr politically. He fled from office; blamed the media for taking "the fun out of the job."

Burr was relieved to leave politics behind—the mean-spirited charges of being "a colorless wimp." Even his mother, coming to his defence once said, "From what I read in the paper, he's lazy, and painfully boring."

Public life robbed him of his dreams. It ruined him politically. Perhaps even destroyed his 21-year marriage to Ruth, with whom he had raised a family of four children.

Candid and open about what has befallen him, Burr explains how life without work nearly killed his spirit. Resumes were dispatched all over Canada. He also went back to school to get a diploma in municipal administration. It seemed nothing helped, including his mayor's credentials. In that period, he became a "stay-at-home-dad."

Suddenly with the casino running full tilt, Burr signed up—along with his ex-wife Ruth and daughter Laura—for the dealer's course at St. Clair. Up until last month, he and his first wife had also been living together for about a year. Although they've just separated again, Burr maintains, "She's my best friend."

As he pushes an empty coffee cup away, getting ready to leave, Louie struggles with a screwdriver to get Burr's picture off the wall. He wants an autograph. In his food-spattered apron, Louie hands Burr a spiffy fountain pen. The former mayor writes his name carefully. But Louie wants more, "Write something there, like 'To Louie, from a former mayor . . .'"

Burr dutifully writes whatever Louie wishes. He grins—it's like he's just stepped back into the past. The happy days. [Jan. 28, 1997]

LET ME CALL THIS FELLOW JEFF, because he asked me not to use his real name.

Yet he wanted his story told.

It's a story out of an era when you couldn't walk into an automobile dealership in Windsor and buy a new car and drive it away.

You could always buy a used car. Or put down a deposit, and order the car of your dreams, but you were warned it might take two to three years before you'd ever see it.

Jeff was 21 in May 1946, when he landed in Windsor. He had just returned from serving in the RCAF during the Second World War. He left his father's farm near Courtright, Ont., and found a job selling furniture at Bernhardt's on Wyandotte. One of the first things he did was head downtown. He was obsessed with purchasing a new maroon-coloured Mercury with twin wiper blades. He had saved $1,500. The salesmen at Noble Duff, however, weren't entirely interested.

Jeff, like so many others, slapped down a $100 deposit, and the salesman agreed to let him know when the car would be in, but warned him not to expect it "for a couple of years." Still, the young man made a point of dropping in once a week. His impatience got the better of him, and he went around to the Plymouth dealership and put down $100 on a new car there.

After a few weeks, he handed over another $100 deposit to the J. T. Labadie's Pontiac dealership.

"I was told the same thing: 'We'll call you! Don't call us!'"

Jeff then paid a visit to the Studebaker dealership on Mercer Street, and gave them a $100 deposit.

"I don't know why—I just I thought I needed a new car that badly. But really I didn't need a car at all—I just thought I did, and I wanted one."

Then off he went to the Nash dealership and forked over another $100 deposit.

"I liked the Nash—my father had a 1927 Nash and I learned to drive in that car on the farm."

The shortage of cars was due to the fact that during the war, car plants had built only military vehicles. Manufacturers returned to full production as quickly as possible, but new designs were long in coming, and buyers like Jeff had to wait. Meanwhile orders for new cars were stacking up with no firm promise of delivery. So now Jeff had five deposits on five different dealerships.

"My heart was set on getting the Mercury—a maroon one. That's what I really wanted," Jeff said.

By November, he was still without a car. To further complicate matters, a tire strike occurred; and now car companies were building vehicles, and shipping them to dealerships without tires. The Mercury dealership—frustrated by Jeff's weekly visits—told him even if they could get him a new car, he couldn't get one with tires.

Undaunted by this, Jeff crossed the river to Detroit, and made the rounds to the tire outlets.

"I found two the right size, but they didn't match. I think I paid $19 apiece for them. I still needed two more."

Jeff hopped on a streetcar that took him to Gratiot and Six Mile in Detroit where he found two more. He piled them into a cab and headed for the border.

"But I had to wait for a cab from Canada to pick me up. I sat on the tires and waited for a cab and then went right back to Noble Duff's.

"The guys there were sitting with their feet up on their desks, and probably saying, 'That's the fellow who keeps bothering us.'"

Sure enough, Jeff got his Mercury.

"It was $1,314 and no tax. A two-door stick shift."

After clocking five months and 3,000 miles on it, Jeff realized that he could sell it for more than he paid, because of the severe shortage, and wound up letting it go for $2,000. It was about that time he met the woman he would marry. He bought a 1938 Plymouth but it broke down on the way to Courtright.

"I was bringing her to meet my parents."

Jeff went back and collected the deposits from the other dealerships so he could come up with enough money to buy a house.

"I bought a bicycle after that, and that's what we used."

Jeff didn't buy a new car again until 1965. [Jan. 26, 2006]

Seeing Dief

[John Diefenbaker]

SITTING WITH FRIENDS THE OTHER DAY and chatting about the political scene in Ottawa got me thinking about the years when Lester Pearson's minority government held on for dear life in the mid-1960s. For some reason, in the spring of 1964, I decided to hitchhike to Ottawa to meet the new prime minister. He had just defeated John Diefenbaker the year before in a hard-fought election campaign, and was handed a minority government.

My goal was to stop in and visit all the leaders of the political parties. It never occurred to me this might be impossible. I never bothered making appointments. I naively figured I'd just stroll into their offices on Parliament Hill and introduce myself. A 17-year-old nobody.

In those days, security was virtually non-existent. I started with Tommy Douglas, and after about 10 or 15 minutes found him in a tiny office. He was gracious and accommodating, and I remember that when he talked he'd cock his head back and stare through a set of very large bifocals. He gave me an autographed picture and told me that by the time I turned 30, there'd be an NDP government elected in Canada.

I smiled, thinking to myself, the day that happens my family will move out of Canada. They had voted Liberal from the days of Laurier, though my grandfather broke rank and voted for Dief in 1958. So did most of the country.

Next in line were Réal Caouette and Robert N. Thompson, both with the Social Credit Party. Caouette seemed to talk about a hundred miles an hour. He sat behind his desk, his arms flailing as he spoke about a strong Canada. Thompson is someone I barely remember except that he handed me a green coloured book (party colours) that explained how the party would print money when Canada ran short. At seventeen, that sounded like a good idea.

The next was the prime minister.

I didn't see him that first afternoon, so I went by 24 Sussex and actually knocked on his door. Nobody answered. I half expected

Pearson would fling open the door, and I'd see him wearing that trademark bow tie. Didn't happen. It occurs to me there is no way I could do this today. I still wonder where security was. I strolled up to the house like it was in any other neighbourhood. Not a soul around. I even peered in the windows.

I caught Pearson in a corridor the next day in the House of Commons. He was in the middle of a conversation when I sauntered up, excused myself and asked if I could have a word with him. Then—and only then—a bodyguard blocked my way, but Pearson waved him off.

I introduced myself, and told him my family knew Paul Martin. We spoke for about five minutes, and he laughed when I told him I had stopped by his house, but he wasn't there.

"Well stop by anytime!" he said with a laugh.

My final objective was to meet the new Leader of the Opposition, John Diefenbaker. I found his office easily enough, but his secretary discouraged me, saying he was "a very busy man," and that unless I had an appointment I couldn't see him. I persevered, telling this woman I'd made such a long trip, just to see him. At which point, Diefenbaker, overhearing my pleas, called from the other room, "Who's out there?" Then he appeared at the doorway to his office.

Without a moment's hesitation he invited me to sit down for a chat. I was especially eager to pepper him with questions from Peter Newman's controversial book *Renegade In Power*, but Dief sidestepped these with his own questions. He wanted to know all about how I had come to Ottawa. He then started in with one personal anecdote after another, steering clear of anything political.

"The name 'Gervais,' I know that name. I defended a Gervais . . ."

"You did? What did he do?" I asked.

"That was one case, I lost . . . and I am sorry to say, he was hanged!"

And so the conversation went. Tales upon tales. And never a word about the dreaded Liberals. Or Dalton Camp. Or any other enemies.

Then a photograph was taken of me, standing with Dief under a painting of Sir John A. Macdonald.

I could've listened for hours.

Today, what Prime Minister or Leader of the Opposition would take the time to talk to a boy of seventeen? In the middle of a busy day? In the midst of a government about to fall?

Not a chance. [Feb. 17, 2006]

A Hanging

[Bruno Kisielewski & Steve Ogrodowski]

I HAD HEARD THE STORY, and forgotten it until a colleague reminded me of it the other day. I'm talking about the last execution in Windsor, when two Detroit murderers went to the gallows in August 1943.

The two men had killed restaurant owner Joseph Borg in his Wyandotte Street establishment in October 1942. Bruno Kisielewski and Steve Ogrodowski, both in their early 20s, spent 101 days in their jail cells before being hanged.

The grim details of that story were recorded by former *Windsor Star* editor Norm Hull, who at the time was a reporter. At the last minute, journalists were barred from attending the hanging, but were there outside the jail waiting with some 200 to 300 people to get the story. The hanging took place after midnight.

The curious thing about the story of this hanging was that after reading it, you are left wondering about the insistent denials made by Kisielewski over his part in the killing. He claimed repeatedly that he had never been to Canada at all, that he'd been framed for this killing. He was the only one of the two to leave letters behind addressed to his family and to his girlfriend, Jonnie. Hull quotes from those letters where Kisielewski tells his girlfriend that he was innocent, and that he would "die an innocent man."

He writes, "Please don't cry about this. You believe I am innocent and always did, so please don't worry about me."

Kisielewski also writes about his mother who had died when he was just a boy. "Now I have a chance to see her . . . I am happy because I will see my Ma again and that I am innocent and I will always be that way . . . I will be with Ma now so nothing will harm me ever again."

Jonnie apparently showed up at the jail the day before Kisielewski was executed, but was denied entry. She had inquired about the man she loved, the man she called "Barnie."

Kisielewski was the first to be hanged. Stepping out of his cell and being led to the scaffold, he said to the guards, "I am innocent and ready to die." When the sheriff A. A. Marentette asked if he had any final words, Kisielewski said humbly, "I'm ready to go." En route to the scaffold, the accused paused at his buddy's jail cell. Ogrodowski reached through the bars to shake his hand.

"No hard feelings," he said to Kisielewski.

"See you later," replied Kisielewski, who was then led to the room where two ropes, each with nooses, hung from the steel rings embedded in the ceiling. The wooden trap door was set over the hole made by removal of slabs of the stone flooring. A Basilian priest met with both men before they took that final walk, then followed the accused to the gallows with prayer book in hand.

Wearing a white shirt, open at the neck, blue denim pants, socks and shoes without laces, the six-foot-four Kisielewski mounted the 15 steps to the gallows' corridor. His hands were bound behind his back. A black mask was slid over his face and the noose slipped around his neck. His legs were strapped together. The hangman—dressed in a tuxedo—hit the lever.

As Hull wrote: "There was a dull thud as the trap door sprung open . . . The sliding rope jerked in a stop, shook momentarily and then swayed gently." Forty seconds had passed from the time Kisielewski left his cell to the time the lever was activated.

Ogrodowski was next. He lit up a cigarette seconds before taking his turn down the corridor. He asked the county sheriff to take it from him only at the last moment, just before the hood was slid over his head. With a cigarette dangling from a corner of his smiling mouth, a swaggering Ogrodowski nodded goodbye.

This was the last execution, but as you read the account in this paper from 1943, you are left wondering about Kisielewski. You are left wondering what sort of peace he had made with himself, with his God, in those final moments.

Two men going to their death. One feeling the need to set things straight; the other worried how long he could keep smoking. [Mar. 20, 2003]

Honouring The Dead

[Hook and Ladder Club]

IF YOU'VE EVER BEEN TO THE Hook and Ladder Club on Seminole Street, you might have seen the memorial to firefighters who lost their lives in the line of duty.

Eight are honoured, and the plaque carries the photographs of all but three.

The other day when I wrote a column about the Royal Canadian Regiment searching for the identities of those in a photograph taken during the Boer War in South Africa, I got a call from a Windsor firefighter. For years, he has proved unsuccessful in his attempts to get a photograph of a firefighter who lost his life in a brutal fire in 1901. He had been a volunteer with the former Walkerville Fire Department. The firefighter who died was Lt. G.R.S. Phillips. It's likely he's one of the eleven shown in the picture that appeared in Wednesday's paper.

But once again, for Andy Meloche, it's a reminder of the frustration he's suffered since he set out on his mission to honour Windsor's dead firefighters.

"I just couldn't seem to get anywhere with this."

He said if there was some way of identifying Phillips in that picture, he'd be able to copy it, and place it on the plaque.

"I've tried everything, but haven't gotten anywhere."

What little is known about Phillips is fascinating. He perished in an explosion at a Walkerville match factory. He had been holding a ladder at the base of the western wall of the building. When the wall collapsed, a huge bridge, which joined the warehouse to the factory, plummeted on top of him. Phillips was struck in the head and shoulders. His back was broken. He lay crushed under a heap of bricks.

Phillips was face down when found by John Taylor, a fellow firefighter, who spotted his boots protruding from the rubble. As the record reported, "It was a pathetic sight and the stalwart firemen were visibly affected. While they carried the corpse to a room in the factory, they could only say: 'The poor fellow! It's too bad, too bad!'"

It wasn't long before the undertaker Odell pulled up with his wagon to remove Phillips from the scene. The veteran firefighter died in that fire along with a man who lived in the same rooming house with him, a Capt. William Brindle.

His picture is also missing from the plaque at the Hook and Ladder Club.

Phillips was 28 at the time of his death. He was a single man, and the son of a clergyman from England. He had just returned from the Boer War. When he answered the call to join the battle there, he left the militia unit, the 21st Essex Fusiliers.

Phillips, described by the old Evening Record as a "popular young man and a courageous fireman and soldier," had returned to Walkerville, but was unable to find work.

The English-born Phillips had been in the employ of Parke Davis and Company, but because of a slight paralysis in his leg, he couldn't go back to work there. The Windsor company however had been gracious enough to keep him on payroll all the time he was fighting in South Africa.

Walkerville had become Phillip's home. He had lived there for about five years, and before that in Leamington. His friend, Brindle, was 38, and hailed from Cardinal, Ont. He had worked as a shipping clerk at Parke Davis with Phillips. He was also part of the 21st Essex Fusiliers, but unlike Phillips had not gone to South Africa. At Phillip's funeral, it is said that several thousand turned out for the event. His casket was draped with the Red Ensign, and pallbearers included six men he had fought with in South Africa. All through the night before, a sentry stood guard over their dead comrade.

In the midst of writing this, an e-mail arrived from a man, pointing out how the *Star* ran this picture, Sept. 4, 1954, identifying nine of the soldiers. It's hoped, from Meloche's point of view, the two un-identified soldiers would include Phillips.

It would put a close to this odyssey toward honouring this turn-of-the-century firefighter. And it would open a door to a part of Windsor's past. [Apr. 23, 1999]

A Forgotten Hero

[Stjepan Hrastovec]

SINCE HIS DEATH LAST MARCH, I've wanted to write about this man. He was the subject of one of my columns a few years ago when friend and Windsor lawyer Peter Hrastovec told me about his father. At first, I thought it was just the usual sort of pride one has for one's father.

So I agreed to meet this elderly man, a former janitor and supervisor of maintenance at Hotel Dieu-Grace hospital.

What I found in Stjepan Hrastovec was a blue-collar intellectual, someone for whom recreation meant lounging in the afternoon and reading Cicero or Pliny or stories of Caesar's wars—all in Latin.

In the eyes of those around him—at the hospital—he was defined by his job. He worked in housekeeping from about 1951 to 1974 when he retired.

What many people didn't realize was that this man, who was born in Croatia and arrived here from post-war Europe, was fluent in five languages. They also were unaware that not only did he write poetry, but also that in his native country he was revered as among the great Croatian writers of the 20th century.

Yet in Windsor, on Bruce Avenue, where he lived, he was simply a labourer, someone who lived and worked in the neighbourhood.

The day I was there, he imparted to me a wisdom learned from a rich life—a life of defying Nazi occupiers, working as a war correspondent in Budapest, and after the war completing his law studies in Austria before coming to Canada penniless.

He told me the most important thing for anyone was recognizing the goodness in one's life, and then living that to the fullest.

As I recall that day, Stjepan led me upstairs to his place of retreat—a tiny cubbyhole that was shadowed by a sprawling maple in the front yard. There in that room Stjepan would immerse himself in the Roman language, imagining himself in a time and place far removed from the quotidian of retired life.

Stjepan Hrastovec was 92 when he died of lung cancer. I remember him as broad shouldered with large, tough hands, and a stare that sized you up in a second.

It was there on that street, not far from Hotel Dieu-Grace, that he raised his family, and that he shared with them his love of literature and religion. Stjepan never owned a car, and so on Sundays he would take a taxi to St. Alphonsus Church downtown.

In a way his children knew nothing about him, except that he worked at the hospital, and that at night, at the dining room table, he would pore over a notebook and scribble down poems. They thought nothing of it.

In his native country—Croatia—Stjepan was revered. He was considered a respected journalist and poet before the Second World War. It wasn't until after the fall of communism and the emergence of democracy that his work started to appear again in journals and anthologies. It precipitated a flood of letters and phone calls from friends and colleagues who had believed Stjepan had died, perhaps during the war.

He was also invited back to his homeland for a reading tour, but declined because of his wife's illness.

If it hadn't been for the war, things might have been different for Stjepan, who published nine books of poetry. His last book—*The Selected Poems*—appeared in 1993. He's also been the subject of some 35 articles in Croatian newspapers and journals. It was his wife and soulmate who typed out everything for him on a portable Remington. She passed away in 1993.

Unfortunately his suppression by the communists eclipsed what notoriety he had in his own country before the war.

He told me, "It was like I was in a grave—buried. People thought I didn't exist."

Yet Stjepan never felt cheated by life. He came to Canada to work hard and raise a family. He never regretted it.

Never for a moment.

He was truly a model.

At the end of his life when his eyes gave out, and he could no longer read, he was not bitter. After all, Stjepan told his family: "I have read almost everything I wanted to read. Am I not lucky?" [Oct. 9, 2002]

The Illiterate Young Girl Who Was Terribly Shy

[Marie Anne Mineau]

WHEN I THINK OF LITERACY, I THINK OF A YOUNG GIRL, terribly shy and skinny, standing awkward and alone in the schoolyard at St. Angela's on Erie Street. I think of the other kids in the yard pointing at her, making fun of the way she spoke, and her clothing, the long dresses and stiff shoes.

It was better she didn't speak. Deep down, she wished she could have disappeared into the clouds above the schoolyard.

I think of the unyielding nuns making her stand by her desk, and repeat after them, and the class laughing at her fractured pronunciation. I think of the assignments she handed in, and the red marks scrawled over them, and how she felt crushed and humiliated. And how she walked home alone along Erie to Gladstone to the red-brick house where her mother waited. And how she envied the other kids who skipped in twos and threes back to their homes.

Marie Anne was from the farm. From Pointe-aux-Roches. She was 11 or 12, and had only heard English spoken maybe at the gas station in the village when someone from Windsor stopped by on their way to London. Or maybe at the farm when someone from the city drove in to ask for directions or to buy eggs. In those instances, it was usually her mother or older sister who handled such transactions.

The year was 1927.

Week by week, and month by month, Marie Anne learned the language. She remained withdrawn and alienated from the other kids in the school. She continued to study. She pored over the *Border Cities Star* when her father picked up the paper on his way home from the Ford Foundry. She yearned for the farm, for the one-room school, for the simplicity of life there. But she was determined to learn English, and borrowed magazines from the barbershop down the street and read every word. Indeed, she read everything she could lay her hands on. In three months, she had a pretty good handle on English, though at times she would slip back, maybe mispronounce a word or employ the wrong verb or noun to describe something. It was about this time that she also overheard the word "illiterate" for the first time. She was

127

described that way by the nuns when they were speaking to the priest who stopped by the school to talk to the class in early September.

She cried when she found out what it meant, and was determined to turn things around. After all, she wasn't *illiterate.* She could say her prayers in French, read the Latin in the mass books. She could also write in French. It's just that she didn't know English.

However, by spring Marie Anne had a pretty good handle on the language, and decided—much against her older sister's advice—to enter the school's public speaking contest. If she won she would be awarded a gold medallion from the local bishop.

She wrote her speech out at the kitchen table and sat there night after night practicing it. After a while it annoyed her father, who was trying to tune into the prizefights on the radio. And so she would go into her room, and pose in front of the mirror and recite her speech, experimenting with gestures, pretending she was addressing the whole school, and the bishop in particular.

Meanwhile, her sister would roll on the bed behind her, struggling to hold back her laughter. From time to time, she would sidle up to Marie Anne: "Marie Anne, there's no way you'll win—you'll be the laughing stock of the school! And I don't want them to make fun of you anymore. Please don't!"

Marie Anne was undaunted. Every night, the same routine. Every night in front of the mirror, rehearsing her speech. Every night perfecting her pronunciation, and hearing her own voice rise and fall, and paralleling each salient point with the proper gestures.

Finally the night of the competition. Four girls in the running. One by one they went up on stage, and delivered their well timed and meticulously prepared speeches.

It was then Marie Anne's turn. She was last.

Her teacher—an older nun who didn't hold out much hope for Marie Anne—whispered, "You know, it's not too late to back out! Don't make a fool of yourself."

She shook her head, mounted the stage, and started in with her speech. She thought she was going to faint. She noticed her classmates snickering and commiserating amongst themselves. She spied her sister rolling her eyes in frustration. She considered bolting for the door and making a run for it.

But her animated words were already filtering into the air.

It was a speech about respect, valuing those less fortunate.

The message came through loud and clear to the students who by the time she had finished had jumped to their feet to applaud Marie Anne.

She had won them over.

The bishop rushed to the stage, and pumped her hand in admiration, and told her she had won the medallion, and that he would drop it by the school the next week and present it to her.

That was my mother. And that day, my mother—Marie Anne Mineau—felt vindicated.

I think of her today, that skinny young farm girl from St. Angela's I have seen in the sepia-toned photographs.

The curious thing is that a year before my mother died, she told me that story, and pointed out to me how the bishop must have forgotten, because he never came back to the school with that medallion. [Sept. 25, 2003]

Love Of Song Backbone Of Group

[Coro Italiano / Windsor Italian Men's Choir]

I'M MET AT THE DOOR BY THE GARRULOUS DOMENICO. He's wearing a plaid shirt. A glasses case bulges in his breast pocket. He's already talking as he opens the door. I feel welcomed. I feel like family. His wife Anna-Maria is also talking. A barrage of words. Some in Italian.

I feel I've come home.

A few others mingle in this basement room where the men of Coro Italiano, or the Windsor Italian Men's Choir, are meeting. I was here four years ago when my editor dispatched me to write a story about this group. I remember promising my wife I'd be back home in an hour or so—I didn't think it would take long. As it turned out, I was there most of the night, eating capicolla and drinking homemade wine. This time around, I've made no such promise to my wife. I've simply told her: "I'm going to Domenico Sansotta's—I have no idea when I'll be back."

Domenico retreats to the lower basement of this house. I can see him in the room below. I smell the garlic. He's cutting up bread, and Anna-Maria is gathering up the trays of salami and prosciutto. The men are meeting here. They're here to discuss plans for next year's 40th anniversary of the choir. They're planning to produce a compact disc. Someone has brought an old vinyl record and throws it on the table, and wonders when this was produced.

A lot of hand gestures, and talk fail to offer any clues. No one knows for sure where it came from, or where and when it was recorded.

The wine arrives, bottled in old whiskey bottles with the labels still attached. Glasses disappear into hands. More talk. More laughter. Someone teases Emmanuele Asciak: "Hey, you're not even Italian." He shakes his head. He's from Malta. He's going back home in a few months.

Renato Chemello wonders about his brother, Luigino, and why he hasn't come from the car. He gets up, excuses himself and leaves by the basement door. The talk continues. It gets louder. I tell them, "This must be like the Italian parliament!"

130

No one seems to agree with anyone.

At one point when Tony Colarossi, president of the Coro Italiano, appeals to them over some issue, he's got everyone on side, till someone at the end of the table, shoots back, "I won't do that!"

Excited words fly back across the table. But there are no hard feelings. This is life. Then the trays of food are placed on the table, and things quiet for a moment as hands reach out for the prosciutto.

Then there's a toast and glasses clink at the centre of the checker tablecloth. I study the hands of these men. These are not the hands of musicians or singers, but men who work hard, men who left behind their homeland with a dream, hope in their heart, and a desire to make a new life here.

This is what this is all about. This choir in this town.

It's about food and wine and talk and song.

One by one they break into song. The songs of their homeland, the songs of their youth.

These are men who put aside their livelihood to meet on Sundays at St. Angela's on Erie Street, or at each other's homes. They seek camaraderie, the gathering of friends, the sticking together, the pride in their roots, their culture, their past. There's a strength here. There's also joy. These men have fun. They love to sing. As evidenced from the summer of 1997 when they swarmed into St. John's to celebrate the 500th anniversary of the arrival of Giovanni Caboto in North America. They stopped traffic as they sang in the streets.

Renato has returned with Luigiano. Somehow Luigiano was locked in the car outside, and couldn't get out of this electronically secure automobile.

Everyone has a good laugh over this. Luigiano reaches for a glass of wine.

And so the night goes. At one point, Tony Colarossi stands up to make a speech, and someone remarks in fun: "If we meet at my house next time, I don't want you to make the same speech again!"

By the end of the night, they're all singing. It's nearly 11:00 P.M. and Domenico has packaged up some bread and prosciutto and wine for me to take home. [Mar. 26, 2001]

The Odd Couple

[Jasper & Manly Miner]

IN THE LIBRARY FILES OF THIS PAPER, I stumbled across an original typescript—yellowed and crumbly—of the 1944 obituary for Jack Miner. It was written by someone called Aitchison, and in it the reporter said, "Jack Miner is dead, but each morning the beating of huge, string wings drum out a requiem for the departed naturalist . . ."

Oddly enough the same sentiment was echoed when Manly Miner, Jack's oldest son, died in 1985. And today, I am sure those driving by the Jack Miner Bird Sanctuary might read a painful lament in the sound of these Canada geese as they swarm over field and pond.

In a sense, with the death of the ruddy-faced, gregarious Jasper Miner in Leamington District Memorial Hospital, we witness a kind of completion of his father's legacy.

Certainly, the Jack Miner Bird Sanctuary and Museum will continue. And Kirk Miner, Jasper's son, is part of the tradition, working at the sanctuary. But with Jasper—the last surviving son of Jack Miner—passing away, it signals the end of an era.

If you pause and speak to older residents around Kingsville, you'll hear the stories. How the two brothers—Jasper and Manly—had perfected an orchestrated ballet of conservation, nature and tourism. How there was an eccentric and oddly friendly animosity between the two. Jasper was often called "Boy" or "Junior" by Manly, the older brother.

It was Manly who was left at home to run things when his father was away on extensive lecture tours. He was the fastidious, cultured custodian. Tweeds with a bow tie, a red silk boutonniere. The gift of gab. He'd regale visitors with anecdotes about his father. Rarely got to work before 2:00 P.M., but stayed at it till 10:00 P.M. writing to dignitaries all over the world.

There's a story around Kingsville about Manly touring Detroit Tigers hall of famer Ty Cobb around the farm. One of the first things he showed Cobb was his bedroom, where the walls were covered in pictures of Cobb cut out of the newspaper. The next day, Manly accompanied Cobb to Detroit, and sported a Tigers uniform at the ball game and warmed up with the ball players before thousands of fans.

Jasper, by contrast, was that other reflection of his father. He loved the outdoors, being among the geese, and he worked hard at entertaining visitors. He'd mount his motorbike and manoeuvre it over the lumpy field, sending the geese into the grey skies. Children loved it.

The two brothers luxuriated in the shadow of their father who, unwittingly, had determined their lives when he set out those first decoys in the pond of their farm near Kingsville in 1904.

Jack Miner had reasoned if the birds would fly away from a hunter armed with a gun, they might instinctively fly toward the man who offered sanctuary. Little did he know how he would change the course of conservation worldwide.

Jack Miner's boys didn't always have it easy. Some say they had to cower and cover their ears whenever they ventured into town because townspeople—partial to hunting—honked their horns out of loathing for their father's conservationist ways.

I have my own memories of the two. The time Manly answered the phone when I was there, pretending he was a voice on an answering machine: "This is the Jack Miner Migratory Bird Sanctuary. The sanctuary is open . . ."

As he droned on, trying to catch the rhythm and mechanical pitch of a voice on a machine, he outlined in detail the hours the sanctuary was open, and pointed out it was closed Sundays. The person on the other must've uttered, "Closed Sundays? C'mon . . ."

To this, an irritated Manly—forgetting he was mimicking an answering machine—responded, "Yes, we're closed Sundays!"

Jasper was the modest one—dressed for the outside, wearing faded corduroys and bulky cardigans, and exuding a kindly, placid presence. The last time Jasper was at his sanctuary was last fall. Barely able to walk, he sat in his car beside the road, silently watching the geese. He sat there for hours. One can only wonder what passed through his thoughts. All the years he entertained the crowds that came there on Saturdays. He loved the people. He loved what he did. He didn't talk about it much. He was a man of action. He didn't desire the attention

Manly did. He wasn't one to deliver lectures. His greatest love was out there in the field.

"They were always in his thoughts," says his daughter, Marilyn Hageniers.

"Even recently in the hospital, in those hallucinations from the pain medication, my dad was dreaming of eagles and geese."

The thing I remember most about him is a photograph of four-year-old Jasper playing with robins around a birdbath, one bird sitting on his shoulder, another fluttering in his hair.

An appropriate portrait of this gentle, humble, soul—the heartbeat of respect for nature and humility. [Jan. 22, 1997]

Follows Famous Father's Footsteps To Claim Prize

[The Younger Paul Martin]

HE NEVER REALLY GAVE IT MUCH THOUGHT when he'd finish work on a hot summer afternoon, step out on Walker Road and hitchhike 30 miles home. He never told anybody that someday he'd get into political life. Indeed, he never really talked politics. He certainly never told anybody he was Paul Martin's son. Not that he kept it secret. It just never came up. He'd climb into the car, lunchbox on his lap, and settle back for the ride to the lake where the Martins had a cottage.

It also never came up when he stuck out his thumb one day, and headed across Canada to go work as a roustabout in the oil fields out west.

The young Paul Martin's mind back then was set on seeing the country, getting a job, being independent.

I spoke with him Thursday from Ottawa, about his days in Windsor, about his mom, and those years spent in the shadow of his father, the late Paul Martin Sr. He's thinking about this now, because Sunday he will be back in Windsor to receive the same award his father was given in 1956.

The young Martin had been there 44 years ago to watch his father receive the Christian Culture Gold Medal Award, an honour that had been accorded to such giants as Nobel Prize winner Sigrid Unset, Henry Ford II and philosopher Etienne Gilson. The young Martin had seen his father in action, heard him speak: "I remember it well, because he was so thrilled to get it."

So in a way, it's a homecoming for Paul Martin, now Canada's federal finance minister, and certainly a contender for the Liberal Party leadership (and much later, the Prime Minister of Canada).

"It means an awful lot, because my father got it, and it certainly strikes an emotional chord, but let me say, it's a great honour, even if I'm not a hometown boy receiving it. That's because the Christian Culture Series is one of the most important Canadian institutions debating Canadian values."

There's no denying that Sunday brings Martin back to his roots here and the stories that surround his family.

"I saw how my mother always made sure my father didn't get too full of himself."

He recounts the story of his mom—Nell Martin—slumping down on a curb at Wyandotte and Ouellette Avenue, while her cigar-chomping politician of a husband went about pumping the hands of constituents. She told him, "I'm not moving from this spot until you stop acting so pompous. About 30 or so people standing nearby applauded."

As he returns to Windsor this weekend, Martin thinks about this, and recalls the constant advice his father gave him, and how he called him twice a day.

The speculation surrounding his own future strikes him as odd. As a boy he never thought about a political career. He never dreamed of being prime minister. His dream—if any—was to work in the Third World. In a way, Martin was never consciously "groomed" to follow in his father's political footsteps. He was too busy pursuing his own life, driving truck for Eastern Construction in Windsor, or working on the fishing boats out of Colchester and Kingsville.

A "normal childhood."

Yet the political education was there. The young Paul—eager for his father's attention—would hop into the car and ride with him as he made the rounds of the riding. As Martin has said before, he never distinguished between his father's triumphs at the United Nations and the routine ribbon-cutting ceremonies. In one interview, he remarked that his father never made "the jump . . . from the post office in Belle River to the podium of the UN."

Martin saw first hand the way things were done. Heard the speeches, saw how the elder Martin met people on their own turf. He learned how his father could feel strongly about what he was doing "on the world stage," because in Windsor or Belle River or Tilbury, he knew he had their support.

"He never forgot who put him there.

"If there is anything to be learned in politics, he said, it's all of that—to be grateful." [May 5, 2000]

McCall Boys See Windsor From Opposite Sides

[Walt & Bruce McCall]

THIS IS THE STORY OF TWO BROTHERS—one who despised living in Windsor and everything about it; the other who raised a family, worked, retired, and now plans to die here. It's a story of contrasts, of looking at life differently. It's about one who discovered something sweet about living on the border, and another who refused to tolerate not only anything and everything about Windsor, but Canada itself.

This is the story of Walt McCall and Bruce McCall. The latter—a successful writer and artist now living in New York—writes for magazines like *The New Yorker* and *Vanity Fair*, and has just published *Thin Ice*, about growing up in Canada. One disparaging chapter, devoted to Windsor, is titled "In Exile."

His younger brother, Walt, once a reporter with *The Windsor Star*, and recently retired as manager of corporate public relations from Chrysler Canada, takes the opposite point of view.

Almost from the moment he arrived here as a boy of 14 in 1953, and within an hour had found an old fire station a few blocks away, Walt McCall's made this *his* home. Older brother Bruce, who sought fame and fortune in the Big Apple, and worked during the glory days for National Lampoon, likened his feelings about arriving in Windsor to the way "Napoleon Bonaparte must have seen St. Helena, with sinking heart and unbearable memories . . ."

The acerbic, older McCall defined Windsor as "a caricature of the Canadian dilemma . . . Windsor found itself geographically and culturally severed from the rest of Canada. It was not quite Canadian and not quite American. It was . . . Windsor."

The family had left Toronto to come here because Chrysler had hired their father as manager of public relations, the same job Walt would fill years later. The family moved to 1793 Byng Road, to a house Bruce McCall describes as "a flimsy reverberating sound box," never intended to accommodate a family of seven. He said this brick bungalow sat on "a patch of grass hardly larger than its shadow, identical to every other bungalow around it . . ."

137

The city, too, gets a knocking: "The motley of squat office buildings and shops dribbling out at the edge of the Detroit River exuded all the glamour, all the pulsing energy, of Gopher Prairie."

Having just finished reading the book, and his brother's words fresh in mind, Walt—once a successful journalist and winner of a National Newspaper Award before going to Chrysler—took a spin by his childhood house on Byng.

It wasn't so bad. Big corner lot. Cute place. Life wasn't so terrible there in the '50s. Sure it was hot and humid, and the ice froze on the inside of the windows in the winter. But . . .

Walt never felt in exile. He saw it as an adventure. He walked all over the city exploring, in particular, the fire stations.

"Where we lived," insisted Walt, "was not quite the ghetto Bruce describes."

But he acknowledged their little house on Byng Road was sandwiched in between a foundry and a stamping plant.

"With the open hearth furnaces of the foundry, the sky was orange . . . And there was volcanic ash all over the neighborhood."

Nevertheless, Walt warmed to the city. Today with fierce pride, he calls it "home."

"I've told Bruce how Windsor gets a bum rap in this book. He's kind of hard on the old place."

Even so, Walt isn't angry over his brother's words. He takes it all in stride. It's partly because "all the bad mouthing about Windsor" has toughened him. Like the time at a Chrysler meeting in Toronto when one woman, upon learning Walt was from here, said, "Oh dear, that's terrible. Windsor's such a dreadful place." He wasted no time in setting her straight. He also once berated a presumptuous CBC camera crew from Toronto that landed here during the tough recession in the '70s, eager to shoot pictures of long lines at soup kitchens.

"I asked them, 'Do you mean the sort of *Brother, can you spare me a dime? stuff?* Is that what you want? 'Yeah, Yeah,' they said. 'Well, you won't find it here!'"

Walt agrees with his brother that Windsor stands alone in the country, that it isn't at all like any other Canadian city. But Walt goes further. It's misunderstood: "It may feel more American, but we have our own identity. And when they say it's a grimy lunch-bucket town, and liken it to Zug Island or Ford Rouge, that makes me mad. It's not. Windsor, with its auto industry, is to Canada what Detroit is to the U.S.

"It's a good place to live." [May 26, 1997]

Painting Herself A Joyful Life

[Adele Duck]

THERE'S ALWAYS BEEN A BIT OF MYSTERY SURROUNDING HER. She's a loner. As a kid she used to spend whole days in the basement, working away with paints and crayons and pencils. Those moments alone would pass one into the other, and watercolour soaked papers would stack up.

And her mother worried.

Adele didn't. She was full of curiosity and enjoyed her solitude. She was lost in the world of her imagination, painting and drawing the world within her.

Today is no different. You might see Adele Duck's name turn up every now and again, especially if you get an invitation to a showing of new work. Or you might run into her at Posteroptics on Wyandotte where she buys frames for her pictures. Or you might find her at the university where she teaches about 12 hours a week.

Beyond that, Adele Duck, whose work has shown in major galleries in Canada and the U.S., works away in a studio just off Wyandotte. A big squarish room that houses nearly floor-to-ceiling paintings. Three pictures stand side by side like skyscrapers in the emptiness of this studio. If the phone shatters the silence—Adele doesn't play music when she's working—she might not pick it up.

There's nobody who can't be kept waiting. This is her time, her moment when she gives herself over to the painting itself, that interior space. It's like the basement of her childhood. As you glance about the room, you make out among the abstract swirls of colour, the figures, the limbs, a glance, a feeling of aloneness. You spot chaos, but what lies beyond is a sense of order.

It says something about Adele herself, her world, a life consumed by work, balancing a university job with her art. In the midst of such demands—a schedule as tight as a family physician's—Adele falls into step, a scheduled work time. An order so defined, some colleagues tell her she defies the stereotype of the artist by keeping *regular* hours.

It's the only way to get things done.

140

And Adele, a graduate of the University of Windsor and Florida State, is working on a deadline to complete a series of 15 paintings for a show that will be traveling across Canada.

The show opens this fall at the Thames Art Centre in Chatham. The first pictures to be framed lean against the wall. There's more to finish. The work certainly reflects her life and while she may have strong opinions, you won't find anything "political," no pronouncements in the work.

"It's too bad, I guess, but I'm really not aware of what's going on most of the time. But I'm no mole in a hole either."

Adele Duck's interest is to reflect "the joy" in her work: "I don't want politics in my paintings. I don't want backstabbing paintings . . . I'd say quality started creeping in."

Such joy has been a part of Adele's life, it seems, since those early years at Hugh Beaton Public School. "We weren't really supposed to learn anything . . . We were allowed to create."

That set Adele loose.

"It sounds so corny, with that little green table and my box of paints, and my mother telling my friends I didn't want to go out and play, but that's the way it was."

But through it all, there's always been an unmistakable joy.

"It's never been a job."

That's why Adele's never compromised herself. Years ago she said, "Other people can paint barns, but nobody else can paint what's in my head and in my gut . . . I'm going to reach fewer people than if I painted barns."

Maybe.

If anything gnawed at her, it was what her mother really thought, whether she worried over her well being in the world.

And when her mother—certainly always supportive—died a few years ago, she finally opened the cedar chest that had been forbidden her as a young girl.

There neatly lay all the ribbon awards for Adele's artwork down through the years.

It was affirmation. A gift. [Jan. 26, 1998]

Cherishing Life's Gifts

[Pat Sturn]

AS YOU STEP INTO THE NARROW LITTLE HALLWAY of this quaint English cottage, you know you're home. You know you're in the presence of someone you like. Even though you've never met her, never known her.

You sit beside the fire, and have a glass of wine and talk about the pictures on the walls, the photographs she used to take, the people she befriended, and what life was like when she first landed in Windsor in the 1930s, an immigrant from Romania.

Pat Sturn is that kind of individual—so giving, relaxed, warm, unpretentious, at ease with the world, at ease with herself.

She speaks in a measured pace like a composer carefully writing out each note of a score. And as she tells you about herself, you recall a story by someone 50 years ago in *The Star* remarking how Sturn's accent gave her voice "a wholly delightful softness and is worth a million dollars in atmosphere."

Maybe. Or is it what she says? Or the way she leans forward in her chair, and tells you things honestly?

Sturn has lived life to the fullest. At 87 she may have slowed, but only just. She doesn't venture out much anymore. "I love my house so much, I don't want to go out." Sometimes she just lies in bed late into the morning listening to music. It's a life with few choices. It suits her mood, this time alone with the things she enjoys, the unique artwork, artifacts and photographs of friends, pictures she took herself.

In another time, Pat Sturn was a human dynamo. From the mid-1930s to 1981 when she retired, she was known for her eclectic talents in painting, sculpting, playing the violin and acting. But her reputation—the real bread and butter—was being among the best portrait photographers in the city.

People who knew her can't forget the rose-peach walls with the elegant accessories that one writer described as being "a self-contained Greenwich Village." The studio was a magnet for those in the know, a gathering spot of artists, writers, photographers, politicians, even kids downtown used to hang out, or run errands, or just sit and talk.

Sturn's roots in this city go deep, to 1934 when she was hired by Will Browne to work in a studio in the basement of the Canada building. She'd come from Europe where she had studied photography and even operated her own studio. At first she had little luck finding a job. But when she spotted Browne's advertisement in the paper, she went to see him. She was hired immediately.

In 1947, Sturn bought the studio from Browne, and from there it took its own shape, the stamp of her own identity.

From the day her mother took her—her hair done up in ribbons, a crisp dress—to a studio to have pictures taken, Sturn always harboured this dream of becoming a photographer. "I loved the thin pencils, and the smell of the chemicals, and the way this man worked."

Sturn's uncle bought her a "pull out" Kodak camera when she was twenty-five. But the business of portrait photography required large format cameras.

"I have really no interest in cameras at all . . . I love to get inside people, to make their life live for posterity. I wanted to take pictures of people to let other people know who they were."

Some have said Sturn was a Karsh in our midst. Always the motivation of doing more, to make something more than just a bridal shot, or a portrait of a lawyer, a child or politician. Like Karsh (who coincidentally did a portrait of Sturn in the 1930s that she carries in her purse) she's cared about making that connection as soon as someone walks through the door.

"I'd never say, 'Smile nicely!' I have to make them forget themselves, get them talking. You have to go by your feelings, or vibes."

In those moments, Sturn soaked up stories of people—their worries and dreams—and her heart went out to them. And they sat honestly for her. Comfortable in her presence. And they told her everything about their lives.

Still, those working years brought moments of terrible concern, like during the war when grieving mothers whose sons had died in Europe would come in to have pictures of their boys copied.

"Mr. Browne didn't want to do it. I didn't either, but I knew we had to."

Mostly the work was uplifting. New friends, engaging conversation, a real seriousness about art.

Sturn feels she's been "lucky" in life, crediting Windsor as helping her realize a dream. "That's what Windsor could do for a little foreign girl who didn't even know the language. I was true to my feelings and to what God gave me. I didn't sit back and say, 'I don't care.'"

Sturn was guided by intuition in her life and work. She listened like a good mother or friend to her clients. Especially the children, who would wait patiently like the tyke Paul Martin Jr., who sat straight and tall for her in a starched white shirt.

Even today, some of those children stay in touch. Now their children mail Sturn crayoned Easter cards.

"I'm everybody's aunt. Even the Lutheran Minister calls me 'Aunt Pat.'"

Those were good years in the studio. Often Sturn wouldn't quit till two or four in the morning. It was her life. It consumed her.

The studio became a place of refuge, of solace. And its memory is still fresh in her mind. "I dream once or twice a week I'm still down there, and that I have never left the studio. I wake up crying.

"I didn't want to be anywhere else. It was lovely. I hardly spent any time in my house, and now look," Sturn adds, her left hand sweeping over the tiny parlour; "I don't ever want to leave." [Apr. 18, 1997]

Plaster Saint

[Don Clarke]

AS I WRITE THIS, I HAVE THE FEELING the late Don Clarke is peering over my shoulder, chomping on a cigar: "You better not make me into some kind of plaster saint!"

Don't worry, Don, the facts speak for themselves.

There are still enough of us around who remember this former Ward 3 alderman who made the present council seem like a pretty lackluster bunch. It was not uncommon, back in the '70s, for the loquacious Clarke to issue blistering diatribes at council—often punctuated by foul language. More than once was he ejected from council chambers for defying the rules by lighting up a cigar.

This newspaper described this feisty city official as someone who, rather than debating matters in an intelligent and logical manner, would resort to "tantrums and hurl invective and scorn upon those who disagreed with him."

The worst of it was a brawl with fellow alderman Roy Battagello that began in a restaurant parking lot and continued later with the two wrestling on the floor of the council chambers.

But talk to the grass roots. Scads of stories in our files quote bartenders, waitresses, lawyers, doctors, educators, policemen, city planners, all of whom claim Don spoke his mind and thanked him for his honesty.

One man said, "Half the guys down there (city hall) don't say what they mean. If they did, the city might be in better shape."

Which leads me to this funny story that I can tell now that Don has passed away. At some point in the late 1970s when many were railing against the growth of the sex industry here, Don suggested some undercover work to check out a downtown massage parlour. Don suspected this place was hawking more than healthy massages.

He convinced the late Bob McAleer—then *The Star*'s managing editor—to dispatch a reporter to the place.

Don decided he ought to come along.

I was the one chosen, handed $65 of *Star* money, and dispatched to join Don Clarke at the Press Club for some strategic planning.

"So I'm supposed to ask for sex?" I asked my editor.

"Ask but don't take!" McAleer snapped back.

Don and I hunkered down over several beers at the Press Club, and after a while forgot entirely what we were supposed to be doing. We argued about everything under the sun, from the myth of high cholesterol and whether cigarette smoke actually caused lung cancer, to Presbyterianism versus Catholicism, and whether the Wings were better than the Leafs, whether Howe was better than Richard, whether Coca-Cola was better than Pepsi . . . You name it.

Finally, we stumbled down the steep steps of the Press Club—then housed in the Norwich Block—and ambled over to this nefarious body rub establishment on Ouellette Ave. Only then did we realize we had failed to agree on a plausible story, and now were being ushered into separate rooms and being told to remove our clothes. The masseuses removed theirs, too.

The body rubs began in earnest.

"Where are you from?" this naked masseuse asked me.

"Toronto," I blurted out.

Unbeknownst to me, Don was saying we were from Kingston.

I told mine I sold insurance. Don said we were geologists.

I only found this out later when we switched and decided to go for the "Roman baths," where the women hopped into a hot tub and lathered us up.

I could hear Don's badgering in the next room. I had chickened out. Couldn't get up the nerve to ask either one of these women if they offered sex on the side. I did learn that one these women was a housewife and mother of two kids.

"What does your husband think of this job?" I asked.

"He thinks I work for Molly Maid."

Don had no such curiosity. I could hear him splashing about, and then suddenly there was a crash. It seems Don had smashed his head in all the excitement and had slipped under water and was now struggling for air. His bathing partner was screaming for help.

I have never seen a naked woman jump as fast as this one, who leapt from the tub—dripping wet—and rushed next door to help resuscitate poor Don.

When his eyes fluttered open, Don was staring at two naked women.

Lucky fellow.

Believe me, I think you staged the whole thing, you devil! [Jan. 24, 2003]

Taking Matters Into Your Own Hands

[Walter Brisebois]

YOU WON'T FIND HIS NAME IN THE HISTORY BOOKS. He's never written a bestseller. He's never won any major awards. He's never led an army into battle. But this man with bulldog determination did wage his own war, and in doing so won the hearts of everybody in this city.

Now with the age-old issue of level crossing delays of traffic being roused again by the recent proposal of CP Rail for an X-ray facility, you might remember that summer of 1969. That's when Walter Brisebois took matters into his own hands, and did what many of us may have wanted to do, but never dared.

That's when Brisebois, a Hiram Walker worker, queued up to a railway crossing—this one at George Avenue—and began to fume. He was on his way home from work. It was a little after midnight. He sat fidgeting and waiting for the train to pass.

Twenty minutes.

Well, he'd had enough. Two weeks earlier he had been held up for 28 minutes. And so when the train shunted out of the way, Brisebois pulled his 1963 Monza Corvair on the freight track. He then stepped out of the car, and stood back and waited. Some fellows from a nearby trucking firm offered him some pizza, and he stood there chomping on the hot pizza and counting out the 20 minutes the train had delayed him. At that point, the CN engine started making its way back. The engineer—seeing the car across the tracks—stuck his head out the cab window and called out, "Are you having car trouble?"

"Nope" shouted Brisebois. "I'm just holding you up for 20 minutes, like you just did to me!"

"You can't do that!" shouted the engineer.

"Just watch me!" bellowed Brisebois, a short squat fellow who refused to be pushed around.

At that point the train engine huffed and puffed and blew its whistle and chugged menacingly toward Brisebois's diminutive Corvair. Then came to an abrupt halt.

The police were dispatched, and Brisebois was ordered to move his car. But he stood his ground, and told the officer he'd lay himself on the tracks if they pushed his car out of the way. Ignoring this, the police had his car towed away, and charged him with "Intimidation." Brisebois spent the night in jail.

The story of this fracas spread quickly, much to the embarrassment of CN Rail. All the television networks had the story. So did *Newsweek*, *Time* and *Esquire*. Newspapers as far away as Louisville, Ky. ran front-page headlines about the "little man" from Windsor who stopped the locomotive.

One headline read: "Man Gets Even With Train."

Everybody vied for an exclusive.

"But I just wanted my story told. I wanted to go to the Supreme Court," says Brisebois, now 70.

He lives in the west end, and hasn't driven a car in 12 years, since arthritis took its toll on him.

Letters of support poured in by the hundreds from all over Canada and the U.S. Some, not knowing his address, scrawled simply, "Train Stopper, Windsor, Ont. Canada" on the envelope.

A man in Detroit lettered the side of his car with the words, "Help Walter!"

Prime Minister Pierre Trudeau wrote Brisebois a letter.

"What did he say?" I asked.

"He said he was 'looking into the matter', like all the other damn fools. I told him, 'You don't need a study—all you have to do is drive up to a level crossing in Windsor and see what's wrong!'"

Thirty-four years later, Brisebois—as feisty as ever—maintains, "Nothing's changed . . . I told them way back then we need overpasses, but, you know what? They've done sweet bugger all!"

It's true—little has changed.

But Brisebois's actions in 1969 epitomized the long-standing fury many have felt as they fall into line day after day and night after night, and wait out the time as boxcars shunt back and forth at Windsor level crossings.

"And so now, do you know what I think? All I can say is this: 'I told you so!'" croons a bemused Brisebois. [Nov. 5, 2003]

A Wag With A Tale

[Ken Koekstat of Crime Stoppers]

THE VOICE. He's sitting at a table at the Back Road Café. His mouth is going a mile a minute. Arms gesticulating. A smile as wide as the table. Ken's telling a story. Customers nearby are leaning in to listen, laughing as Ken takes them through the drama of catching "bad guys."

Ken Koekstat tells a good story. He's Captain Crime Stopper. Heads the Crime Stoppers unit for the Windsor Police, and has since 1989 when he was taken off the street beat. He's deep into a story about a jogger who one morning about 5:30 saw a man lifting a huge picnic table from Memorial Park into a pickup truck. Thinking this looked suspicious, the jogger paused to scrawl the man's license plate in the dirt, then continued on. When the jogger got home, he showered, dressed for work, and drove back to the spot to write down the plate number. Then called Crime Stoppers.

The investigation got stalled when the police couldn't get hold of the man. In stepped Captain Crime Stopper himself. He hopped into his cruiser and drove over to the man's house.

"I'm like a pit bull—I don't give up."

Koekstat gave the man two options: Either return the picnic table to the park, or face arrest.

"I told him we had an eyewitness . . . Of course, I was bluffing—I didn't even have the name of this jogger.

"As you know, every call is anonymous. We don't want names or phone numbers from our callers—just the information . . .

"And so this guy kind of looked down, like they all do when they're caught, and said, 'Okay, you got me!'

"The man then backed up his truck to a row of trees behind his place and loaded the table into it.

"Seconds before he drove away, the thief turned to me and said, 'Can you make sure that when I'm putting this back in the park, the police don't come by and bust me for stolen property.'"

Koekstat has hundreds of stories. And when you wind him up, he starts spinning them out like it's some sort of contest.

"Oh, let me tell you about this one . . ." and he's off again.

His passion for catching bad guys is all consuming. It never fails to bring satisfaction. Sometimes, he's called to it right on the street. Like catching a thief at Sam the Record Man, chasing the man down and making him go back to pay for $154 in CDs he'd stuffed under his coat. Another time—much to the chagrin of his frightened wife—he booted after a hit-and-run guy with the family car.

"They don't know I'm a cop until I stop them, and I say, 'Allow me to introduce myself.'"

Koekstat, who has received numerous citations for apprehending suspects for armed robbery and other crimes, feeds on calls to Crime Stoppers like a hungry dog foraging for scraps. Anything. Anytime.

Those calls to 258-TIPS are what keep Koekstat and his crew on the move. Last year alone, Crime Stoppers paid out more than $47,000 in rewards.

Who's doing the telling?

"I don't care; I don't want to know; we just want the information." Koekstat recites.

There's no caller ID on the phone at Crime Stoppers.

But Koekstat knows many tips come right from the criminals themselves. Often out of spite. Or just to fetch the reward.

Many times, tips stem form people overhearing remarks in a bar. "Someone shoots off their mouth."

Like the time a woman was knocked down and the thief, who ran off with her purse, told a buddy in a bar what he'd done. Another man nearby overheard him.

. "But," says Koekstat, "the guy didn't believe it, until he saw the crime reported in the paper. Then he called us. No one ever said criminals were smart."

Another time, a fellow tried to knock off a bank in Windsor but was met at the bank exit with $14,000 in cash by the Windsor Tactical Squad. "This guy had been bragging about what he was going to do. We were ready."

The stories are endless. It's like that old slogan from the '50s TV cops-and-robbers show: "There are eight million stories in the Naked City."

Captain Crime Stoppers knows them all. [Jan. 8, 1999]

A Bookie Is A Bookie Is A Bookie

[Whitey Benoit]

NOT MUCH HAS CHANGED FOR WHITEY BENOIT. Sure he's moved from roll-your-owns to filter tipped Players, and he hasn't done any prison time in the last 30 or 40 years. And sure, he hasn't been taking in much bookie business. Then again, he's 90 years old.

Whitey still sports the white brush cut. Still the smile, more brilliant than Casino Windsor sparkling on Riverside Drive at night. Still the brash, defiant manner. He could take on the world.

And some ways are hard to change even when age creeps up on you, squeezing the strength out of your legs as it has for Whitey.

But in the bedroom closet, a cardboard box of Black Velvet mickeys shows he's open for business. Whitey hawks the booze to the alkies who know him, and know he's got a supply. And on the tiny desk is the phone. Beside it, the newspaper's harness-racing entries and results.

Where some seniors might while away their retirement wood-carving or hooking rugs, Whitey has taken up bookmaking . . .

He's been at it for four decades and has watched it slow. "The casino is taking all the loose change—business is way down now."

Whitey's doing the horses, takes bets daily. And this weekend, he'll take them for the Packers and Patriots for the Super Bowl. Fourteen to one odds on Green Bay. Personally he couldn't care less who wins. Still he'll be in this sunlit living room of his Glengarry Street flat, sitting by the phone and watching the game on television.

The afternoon I saw him, he was at his window, the curtain pulled back. He opened the door with a greeting in an eager voice larger than a handshake.

He'd been watching golf, warming himself by a small electric heater. He complained about "that damn" fan on the furnace that had given out a while ago.

Whitey—slippers, white socks, a warm sweater—sat on the edge of his couch and offered me a drink. He flicked ashes into a tall brass ashtray with a carving of a race horse.

All his needs were being met. A Swanson turkey dinner warming in the oven, the telephone jangling with business.

These late afternoons he calls his "office hours . . . Right up to post time. "

Whitey complained he only made $30 the night before. There on a white pad is all the action, recorded in a meticulous hand. Mostly he bets the tracks in Windsor and across the river.

"This is my bible!" he declares, thumbing open *The Windsor Star* sports pages. He's referring to the harness racing information it provides daily.

"I don't know anything about these horses, or the jockeys, or anything. I don't need to know anything—except the odds."

Whitey has his regulars, and waits a week or two to collect. They drop by the house: "I got $400 they owe me right now."

Most bets are $20, usually nothing more than $50.

"Peanuts!" scoffs Whitey. "That's all it is. Between this and old age pension, I survive."

Whitey isn't worried about the police knowing: "The coppers know where I am. They know what I'm doing. What are they going to do? Put a 90 year old man in jail?" As for the Super Bowl, Whitey doesn't expect much action. "But if you have a bet, I'll take it. You can be sure of that."

Whitey isn't worried about intruders. He's got a crushing grip, and a 12-inch Bowie knife on a nearby dresser.

"Nobody's going to bother me here!"

Things weren't always so desperate for Whitey. His father had been a millionaire. Money made in the rumrunning business.

As for Whitey, raised in Catholic schools in Toronto and Montreal, he never could go straight. During Prohibition he was running hot diamonds across the border for the infamous Purple Gang in Detroit.

During the 1950s he was described in the papers and the magazines as the "King of the Forgers." He'd developed a Canada-wide scam of cheque cashing that netted him thousands. Also, it landed him in Kingston Penitentiary, twice. Altogether, he spent some twelve years behind bars.

Some still recall this barrel-chested man, who can look as menacing as a linebacker, relaxing in the summer sun at Mercer and Pitt with his diminutive white poodle, Fifi. So gentle was he, they will tell you.

The dog had been left to him by his "lady friend" who lived on the other side of the duplex. Fifi died two years ago.

Whitey, staring out the window at the new casino rising up like a bad dream out of the frozen winter ground, swears he hasn't gotten soft. "You know, I still say my prayers every night," he confesses. [Jan. 18, 1997]

A Man For All Seasons

[Saul Nosanchuk]

HE'S DEFENDED HARD-CORE BIKERS IN WINDSOR COURTROOMS. He's mentored impressionable young lawyers in classrooms. He's been a champion of restorative justice, and when the time came to set a porn star free, he did it knowing it would cause controversy.

In his lengthy career as a criminal lawyer, law professor and judge, Saul Nosanchuk has done it all.

A week ago, we met at a new haunt of his, a restaurant on Wyandotte. I spotted that unmistakable figure—a gaunt, tall, bearded man—loping into the Velvet Diner. It's always fascinating meeting with this Ontario court judge, because the conversation ranges from books and music to regional history and hockey at local rinks. There is nothing that does not keenly interest this 72-year-old, who grew up in Windsor delivering groceries for his family-owned market.

This childhood experience helped shape the way he has governed himself in his career, first as a criminal lawyer and later as a judge. "I could never imagine my parents not caring for any person who walked into that store. We were to be solicitous and concerned and deliver the best possible service.

"That really set the model for me on how people ought to be treated. And as a judge I want people to know that when they walk into my courtroom, we are delivering justice in a calm atmosphere where people will feel they are treated fairly . . ."

Nosanchuk's law career spans 46 years. From 1959 till his appointment as a judge in 1976, he was a criminal defence lawyer. Now, he'll be working as a per-diem judge, which means the Ontario court can call on him whenever he's needed. It means his workload will be lessened as he nears mandatory retirement at 75.

As a youth, attending Assumption University, Nosanchuk toyed with a career in law. Soon after graduation, he was off to Toronto to live in the old Ford Hotel and study under the legendary G. Arthur Martin at Osgoode Hall.

After Osgoode, Nosanchuk returned to Windsor and his career soon gravitated to criminal law. He won't ever forget his first day in the courtroom: "I was so nervous, my knees were knocking."

He remembers fondly a time when a hardened criminal he was cross-examining interrupted the proceedings with a request to check on whether his parking meter had expired.

Nosanchuk had a good laugh. Here was a man convicted of extortion and other odious crimes suddenly worrying over a mere parking ticket.

As a criminal defence lawyer, Nosanchuk had the touch, maintains Harvey Strosberg, his former law partner. "He was one of the best jury lawyers—he could connect with a jury in a profound way. . . . His humility and humanity oozed through."

Strosberg recalls how once in the midst of presenting a case, Nosanchuk dropped all his notes to the floor. "Two jurors jumped right out and helped him pick them up. . . . That was Saul—he connected with everyone."

Nosanchuk's best known case was the murder trial of Matthew Lamb, an 18-year-old, who in 1966 fatally gunned down two people on a residential street and injured a third. The accused was found not guilty by reason of insanity.

To support this claim, Nosanchuk sought the independent opinion of Detroit's Dr. Emmanuel Tanay, one of the leading forensic psychiatrists in the U.S. and someone who had testified in support of the defence of insanity at the trial of Jack Ruby, who was charged with the murder of Lee Harvey Oswald, the assassin of President John F. Kennedy.

As a judge, Nosanchuk is still remembered for dismissing charges against porn star Marilyn Chambers in 1987 for allegedly obscene dancing at a Windsor strip club. Nosanchuk concluded that while Chambers may have been scantily clad during her show, she was not "nude as defined by the Criminal Code."

Nosanchuk's judgement contrasted dramatically with other nudity trials handled by other Windsor judges that had resulted in guilty verdicts for several strippers here.

But as a judge, Nosanchuk has garnered an enormous amount of respect among lawyers. One of Windsor's leading criminal lawyers,

Pat Ducharme, calls him "the model of civility," and someone who has "an immense empathy for both those victimized by crime and the trauma of the accused.

"He teaches lawyers how people ought to be treated."

Strosberg agrees: "Everyone respects Saul. He is someone who marches to his own drum . . . And everybody loves the tune!" [Oct. 13, 2005]

Nitwit Prophets, Dancing
Novelists and a Barber's Son

Writing And Teaching

[Alistair MacLeod]

ALISTAIR MACLEOD STEPS INTO THE ROOM, carrying an armload of his own books. The rugged face of a Maritimer. Jacket and tie. And that mischievous smile.

He's there to meet twenty-one Catholic Central High School students and their teacher. There to chat with them about creative writing, how he goes about the craft, his short stories, his only novel, or anything else under the sun.

And when the amiable MacLeod is introduced as the one who has just been nominated for the $172,000 IMPAC Dublin Literary prize, he quips, "I guess I'm even more famous now than I was 10 minutes ago."

Don't misunderstand. This is no boastful fellow. This is Alistair MacLeod—down-to-earth, warmhearted, generous, someone who genuinely cares about writing, and someone who cares about helping students.

This 65-year-old retired University of Windsor professor and writer steps into the room. Within seconds, he's joking with these high school kids. Then begins showing them the dust jackets of his books, and singles out an earlier book called *Lost Salt Gift of Blood*. Then confides how an editor warned him that it was a difficult title. Too much of a mouthful of words.

"True," MacLeod allowed. "It's the one title no one remembers. They'll say, 'Oh, I read your book . . . you know, the *bloody* one, the Bloody Lost Salt or whatever . . .'"

MacLeod holds up two editions of it, one showing a house or building near the sea with a cow peeking in from one side; the other without the cow.

"What do you think? Cow, or no cow?" he asks. The class votes for the cow. So does MacLeod. Then there are the covers of *Island*, his collected stories. The Canadian edition with a photograph of a spit of land jutting into the lake with a single pine tree. The American edition with "this fat little tree," as MacLeod describes it.

"You see, they've changed the picture—they put this tree in that isn't in the other picture. "What do you think?" The class votes for the first edition.

"I like it, but maybe it's because I saw it first."

A quizzical expression forms on MacLeod's face as he ponders this notion. And remarks, "Isn't this—this idea of changing the cover—a little like painting a mustache or a pair of glasses on someone in a picture?"

They laugh.

MacLeod does, too.

In truth, the cover art doesn't bother MacLeod all that much. He acknowledges he knows nothing about design.

Alistair MacLeod is a man of immense gratitude. Not at all the tireless self-promoter. His forte is writing. He's at home with this. It's what he does best.

And teaching. That's what lured him here today—to share with them something that he learned about the craft of writing. Otherwise, MacLeod wouldn't be here. After all, invitations arrive daily for him to attend literary festivals, to do readings, lectures, book signings, guest appearances. Last month he was featured on the front of the *New York Times Book Review*. His books have won major awards all over the world.

He's just returned from Boston and New York where he was promoting *Island*. It's clear—MacLeod doesn't *need* to talk to this bunch. He *needs* a rest. So why is he doing it? It's because he was asked. Asked only days before and he didn't hesitate to say, "Sure."

It's the teacher side of him that has him talking to these students. He speaks to them about the relationship of a writer and editor: "You (as a writer) may have two or three characters in your novel and you also have this talking bookcase . . . Well, an editor will come along and say, 'This talking bookcase, I don't know about that . . . I don't think it's going to be believable!'

"But as the writer, you say, 'Oh I think it is! I want to keep it!' But as a writer, shouldn't you listen?"

Writers can be difficult? Sure. Is MacLeod? Probably not, though a story circulating about him and his first and only novel reports he was met in Toronto by his editor who practically had to wrench it out of his arms. All because MacLeod felt he needed more time.

True?

Leave that one for legend.

As for the sudden success over the past couple of years, MacLeod takes it all in stride.

"Pizza for everyone here!" he announces to the class. [Mar. 7, 2001]

Barber's Son Listened, Learned

[Salvatore Ala]

HE STROLLED INTO THE WINDSOR STAR one afternoon 18 years ago, sat down, opened up a file of writing, and asked me to scan it. Poetry. Some truly bad; others showing remarkable promise. When he went away I thought this is someone passionate about literature, about words, even to the extent of its geography, or the way they fall on a page, like the arrangement of notes in a musical score.

I was honest with him. Told him to get busy reading. Turned him in the direction of contemporary poets, Patrick Lane, John Newlove, Margaret Atwood. Others. Told him to educate himself. And by that, I meant, see the world, see it through the eyes of other writers, taste it, experience it, think about it.

Earlier this week, tucked in my mail slot was an envelope containing his first book of poems. I opened to the first poem, and was amazed by its maturity, by the erudite gloss. After reading through most of the book, I knew a little more about this person.

Yet I knew nothing. Who is this person? This man with a Renaissance name—Salvatore Ala?

I telephoned him. He was in the midst of fixing some leaky taps in the basement. His wife, Brigitte, a neuro-radiologist, was upstairs asleep.

"I can't disturb her . . . I'll come see you."

He did. He strolled into *The Star* once again, now 39, but a hundred years wiser. Still the handsome face, physique of an athlete, except for a bad knee that ended dreams of being a soccer star.

Then I discover I knew his father.

"A barber."

"Not *Frank* Ala?"

"Yes. He had the barber shop on University, right at the Capitol."

I knew the man well. Would amble in there Friday mornings to get a haircut. Mostly from Joe Belmonte who worked for him. I'd fall asleep as these traditional Italian barbers applied hot towels to my face in preparation for a shave.

"The man's a legend in Windsor!" I said.

Sal seemed pleased.

The family first lived on Glengarry near the present day Casino Windsor. Later, they moved to South Windsor. His father would walk downtown to the shop. As a boy, Sal reaped the benefits of his father's business by getting hockey sticks from Alex Delvecchio, who used to cross the river to Windsor for a haircut. So did Ted Lindsay, and other celebrities.

Frank died seven years ago of lung cancer. The shop closed two weeks later. It wasn't until about 18 years ago, shortly before I met him, that Sal decided he'd become a poet. When he told his father, his father seemed a little disappointed. Thought he should get a real job. But then told him to go see me. Also to talk to Len Gasparini, another poet who grew up in Windsor.

What prompted him to dream of being a writer was finding a copy of John Keats' poetry in a drawer of a cabinet at an antique store.

"I started reading it, and knew then I wanted to be a poet."

Over the next 18 years he started learning the craft. Meeting with Gasparini and Joe Coté, a St. Clair College teacher. They'd stay up till 4:00 A.M. talking about writing. "I learned so much from them."

Then there were Tuesday night sessions at Homer Plante's, a former University of Windsor English professor who inspired so many students. From Plante, Sal learned dedication, the elegance of the craft, its authority and power.

Now Salvatore Ala is giving a little bit back to the world. He's only just begun to write about his father:

> Your spirit, father, was first to die.
> *When the diagnosis came, and doctors like dominoes fell away,*
> You knew—the history of your family was upon you . . .

Sal plans to do more. Remembering the barbershop.

"I think he'd be proud of this," Sal says, holding up a copy of his first book, *Clay of the Maker*.

"I think he would be proud . . . He used to love watching me play hockey and soccer. I know he would've liked this."

Sal, you're right.

He would have sold the book to every lawyer, doctor, banker, and hockey player who stepped into his barbershop. [Aug. 1998]

165

Message Of Genius Lost Amid A Sea Of Gibberish

[Marshall McLuhan]

TWENTY-FOUR YEARS AGO, ALMOST TO THE DAY, a former managing editor of this newspaper dispatched me to run over to CBC and interview Marshall McLuhan.

I stood beside the great writer, while makeup was being applied to his face, and I asked one question only. It doesn't matter what that question was. I don't remember it. All I recall is that it caused a torrent of words. McLuhan never stopped talking. And I never stopped taking notes. McLuhan talked a hundred miles an hour without taking a breath. And this deluge of words washed over me.

Finally, when I stepped outside, I stared at my notebook in bewilderment. None of what he said made any sense. Total gibberish.

"What did he say?" asked the managing editor.

"How do I know? If I told you, you'd think *I* was nuts! The guy's crazy!"

"He's McLuhan! Seer of the 20th century!" thundered my editor.

"A nut case!" I countered, and trundled off to make sense of my notes.

A story appeared. A lame one. That was the only time I met the visionary communications theorist who was forecasting the effects of the electronic media on modern culture as early as 1964.

He was an academic rebel and a brilliant linguist who loved puns and word play. He was the one who coined that famous phrase, "The medium is the message."

For nearly two years McLuhan lived and worked in Windsor. Rev. Stan Murphy, the Basilian priest, was responsible for luring him here. In 1944, Marshall McLuhan, then 33, took up his new position as head of Assumption's English department. He lived in a farmhouse on Tecumseh Road. And it turns out his first adventure in this city was not with his students, but with a cow.

Corinne, McLuhan's wife, had decided to teach the master how to drive a car. Things didn't go well. This is the conversation between McLuhan and Father Stan on the first day of classes:

"I had my first lesson last night . . ."

"And?" says Father Stan.

"And I thoroughly blew it! Big bust! I kept jamming on the brakes and flooring the accelerator. So, Corrine says, 'Well, Marsh, since you can't get out of second gear, perhaps we should try teaching you how to go into reverse.' I couldn't get out of second gear, right? Then she's telling me to go in reverse, right?"

"Right? And?"

"And . . . Well, I backed into our cow, our lovely Jersey cow."

There are more stories: Corrine McLuhan—after selling a double bed the couple had been using—boasted to a young Basilian seminarian how the bed springs never last long on any bed she and McLuhan shared.

Or the tale of McLuhan chasing a tornado along Tecumseh Road. He described a farmer running alongside, and firing shots into the funnel cloud. Meanwhile McLuhan and a buddy were snapping pictures of the tornado.

McLuhan remarked at the time: "We saw it collapse ever so leisurely, beautifully. Like the Indian rope trick. Something out of Arabian Nights. Bee-yoo-tee-full!"

There are stories, too, of McLuhan's parenting skills. How the media prophet whined about how long it took to feed a pair of babies, how he griped about his son's "rambunctiousness." At one point the writer actually bolted a window-screen across the top of his son's playpen to stop him from escaping.

McLuhan also grumbled constantly about how the washing machine was "an invasion in the home, about the way they make people mechanical slaves."

His stay in Windsor didn't last long. In the spring of 1946, McLuhan was offered a job at St. Michael's College in Toronto.

From all reports, McLuhan was a remarkable teacher, but one with unorthodox ways. He never wore socks to class, and would often lean over a colleague's plate at dinner and eat from it.

Eccentric and brilliant.

But the man I met here in 1977 was a babbling nitwit. Then again, maybe I just didn't recognize genius staring me in the face. [Nov. 7, 2001]

Mentor Coming To Dinner

[Miriam Waddington]

AN OLD FRIEND—A WRITER AND MENTOR—died in Toronto last week (March 3, 2005). She was 86. I couldn't help but think about the time when she came to Windsor to do a reading. She had telephoned from the Holiday Inn at the time it was situated downtown on the riverfront.

She had called to complain about how members of the English Department at the University of Windsor had wanted to take her out for dinner. But Miriam didn't want to eat in a restaurant.

"Do you remember when I invited you to my house for dinner?"

I did. Nearly 15 years had passed since I had nervously sent her a letter. I had been living in Toronto, and my letter back in 1965 had praised Miriam's writing, but also asked if she wouldn't mind taking a look at my own poetry. I was barely 19 at the time.

She shot back a note urging me to call her. I did. She invited me for dinner, and after we cleared the dishes, she sifted through the poems I had brought.

"This is absolutely terrible!" she exclaimed, as she flipped through the manuscript. She could find nothing good in what I had shown her—except for one line.

At first, I felt crushed. But then Miriam—still absolutely sincere—zeroed in on that one verse, and told me how it demonstrated to her that while I had failed to write anything to whet her imagination, there was potential.

"I don't know if you will ever be a poet, but this shows potential."

I knew she meant it. And that was it.

"Yes," I told her. "I do remember that dinner."

"So, you remember me cooking for you?"

"Yes," I said.

"Well, I want to see you again, and meet your family and come to your house and have you, or your wife, cook dinner for me! Tonight!"

That night we had the renowned poet and critic Miriam Waddington to our house. We talked for hours about writing. We chatted about some of her old cronies, especially the irascible Irving

Layton, a contemporary of hers from that period in Montreal right after the Second World War. Layton had edited and published Miriam's first book as part of the now-famous *First Statement* series.

I showed Miriam a new book of Latyon's. It was more of the same irreverent and vulgar verse that had brought so much attention to him in the 1950s and 1960s, but was now quickly going out of fashion.

Miriam scanned the poems, occasionally reading a verse out loud, specifically those that had more obvious sexual references. "Oh, Irving!" she lamented. "So pathetic in your old age! Grow up!"

The other thing I remembered from my visit to Miriam Waddington's in 1965 was our discussion about Anais Nin, the Parisian writer who put up the money to publish Henry Miller's controversial book, *Tropic of Cancer*. I had been fascinated with both Miller and Nin, especially her earliest books and diaries. Miriam told me she had met Nin at a conference in Pennsylvania where the two were delivering academic papers on the psychoanalyst Otto Rank, who had studied under Sigmund Freud. Nin also mentions Miriam in the Seventh volume of her diaries and complains about her "negativity" at that conference. The two writers continued to correspond over the years.

Learning of Miriam's death last week prompted me to think back to the times we'd met, and the help she gave me as a writer. Especially her honesty and directness.

And then just the other night when I was driving home, I heard a recording of her reading a poem on the radio. There was that familiar voice—a hint of coyness in the way she formed the words, but with an underlying honesty. Miriam never seemed to despair over old age—it was something she had accepted and rejoiced in. And there was a brashness about her that seemed to suggest: "Why not?" [Mar. 11, 2005]

Sisters Of Wit

[Elizabeth Shaughnessy Cohen & Margaret Atwood]

THEY WERE SISTERS OF WIT. Shaughnessy was a friend. A gregarious, happy friend who made Margaret Atwood—ever the master of one-liners—smile and laugh. The politician and the writer.

The two would gladly engage in a good turn of phrase, a funny anecdote, or indulge in those crazy coincidences and notions that poked fun at traditions, or the way things were. They would stop at nothing, those two. Chatting about everything.

"Writing, books, hairdos . . . What didn't we talk about? Anything you might care to mention!" as Atwood told one reporter last week after Shaughnessy died.

Atwood, while driving in her car, learned about her friend collapsing in the House of Commons and later heard the news of her death. She was stunned. She telephoned me at the newspaper and wanted to know the details of the funeral.

Only 10 days earlier, she had run into Shaughnessy in a parking lot, and was consumed with laughter as she stood there in the December sunlight.

That was the connection—the laughter, the merriment.

"It was one long gag, knowing her," recalled Atwood. "I've known her for so long, before she went into politics . . . She was a lawyer and doing immigration work."

Atwood was first introduced to Shaughnessy through a mutual friend when the writer came to Pelee for bird watching—a passion of Graeme Gibson's, the novelist with whom Atwood lives in Toronto.

Soon Atwood was joining Shaughnessy at her cottage: "I got to know her, and we'd have long chats. You know, she was a practical joker, but more so in Ottawa, and not here, at least not with me. But she was so much fun, so gregarious."

Yet it was readily apparent that beneath that playful mirth, there was a depth, a compassion for others.

Atwood knew that side of her intimately. She was bowled over by the politician's boundless energy, her ability to make things happen, to clear away blockheaded bureaucratic entanglements.

"She had an amazing line of contacts . . . A wall flower, she wasn't!"

Atwood had planned to be in Ottawa next week, and had hoped to get caught up on things.

Saturday at noon was catch up time.

A time to bid a farewell.

It seemed appropriate that the salty-tongued Father Paul Charbonneau would be there to infuse the kind of jocularity that would have warmed Shaughnessy's heart. He certainly had some 800 mourners roaring with laughter at a crowded St. Anne's Church in Tecumseh.

"He's a real pro," Atwood whispered to me in the pew during the service. She was surprised at the applause during a Catholic mass. Only once before had she seen such levity at a Catholic service, when Barry Callaghan stole a jazz band into the church loft to surprise everyone by playing as his father Morley's funeral casket moved up the aisle.

Atwood chuckled at Charbonneau's approach. It fit the mood—it fit Shaughnessy.

In the midst of this, the Toronto writer, who had come with so many others from all over the country, paid a silent tribute to her old friend.

Afterwards at Branch 12 of the Royal Canadian Legion, near some of Shaughnessy's old haunts, like the Victoria Tavern, the writer sat on a chair balancing a cup of coffee and a plate of flood, and spoke to the people—those from Pelee Island, the old neighbourhood, the close friends, all who knew and loved her friend.

She also spoke at length with some Bloc Quebecois members, and learned just how far Shaughnessy's net of goodwill had spread.

Atwood wasn't surprised. "She knew so many people."

It was important to be there, to bid farewell.

And moments before leaving the Legion hall to return to Toronto, Atwood, draped in that characteristic long cloak, paused to one side of the Shannon Brothers, a lively Celtic band, and moved and turned gracefully to the music, absorbing its jaunty perky style.

Sometimes words are not enough. [Dec. 14, 1998]

The New Skates

[W.O. Mitchell]

WHEN W.O. MITCHELL TOLD THE UNIVERSITY OF WINDSOR in 1986 that he was resigning as writer-in-residence, he wasn't entirely eager to return to his home in Calgary. Life had been comfortable here, living on the west side in a small apartment and being driven to his Sunset Avenue office by his wife Merna each day.

It was more her wish than anything, and the reason was a simple one.

Mitchell had been here eight years, and had produced more during that time than at any other period in his career. By his sixth year, he had already pounded out three books, two new stage plays and a feature film. By his eighth year, he had completed yet another novel, and was making notes for more.

Life was good.

The typewriter clacked in his office.

As I read through *Mitchell: The Years of Fame 1948-1998* it brought back memories of the writer in Windsor.

I met him that first fall in 1979 when he accepted the writer-in-residency at the English Department. Alistair MacLeod had suggested Mitchell be considered after Joyce Carol Oates' departure. In those first months Mitchell lived the life of a vagabond, moving from university residence to hotel, and then coincidentally to my house where he stayed until Christmas break.

How had this come about? One night at a dinner party, he was complaining about living in a hotel when my wife, Donna, offered an extra bedroom in our house. Mitchell accepted, without batting an eyelash. I quickly reneged, informing him I had young kids at home. Brats, really. High-pitched brats.

"I love kids," he cut me off.

"The kids are always sick, colds, flu, skin diseases . . ." I protested.

"I never get sick," W.O. shot back.

The next day W.O. moved in. Within a week, he was crippled with a severe cold. I'd find him at night slumped sullenly in an armchair with that silent mean scowl on his face. He'd sit there in my living room all day long feeling sorry for himself. But as soon as the children returned from school, Mitchell's spirits soared. He did magic tricks, played word games, spun wide-eyed yarns, or settled down with my oldest boy, André, for whom he had special affection.

A few years later, when CBC asked Mitchell to do a Christmas show reading a story from his popular Jake and the Kid, he asked me if Andre would take part in the show. But my son was terribly shy and refused. Mitchell, undaunted by this, said, "Let me ask him." And he did. He asked Andre:"What do you want most for Christmas?" Andre didn't miss a beat:"A pair of Bauer Supreme Skates, size 7!"

Mitchell said, "If you go on this show with me, and by the way, you don't have to say a thing, just sit there and pretend you're interested, I'll make sure you get those skates." Andre agreed. And Mitchell went back to CBC and negotiated as part of his contract a pair of size 7 Bauer Supreme.

A month later, Mitchell found a seat at the frigid Adie Knox Arena near the university and cheered as my eight-year-old son—scoreless at that point in the season—suddenly came alive, and scored five goals.

Mitchell was on his feet shouting: "It's the skates! I got'em those skates!"

Mitchell was Windsor's darling. It was in this city that he hit a new stride, writing like there was no tomorrow.

At the university, his door was always open, and often he held court in the hallway. He loved to talk. So much so, however, say his biographers, that after a while the profs started shutting their doors because they knew "a promised 10-minute reading from him could easily turn into a two-hour session."

Tom Dilworth, a professor in English, was "one of Bill's frequent captives. He described Mitchell "as an Ancient Mariner monologist—dramatic and compelling, but very time-demanding."

Mitchell felt at home here: "He could be heard banging away on the electric typewriter (he destroyed three typewriters in Windsor alone) from about eleven to four every day, including Saturdays and Sundays. Quite soon his office took on the Mitchell ambience of brown snuff and tea stains. Pungent eucalyptus scent and brown smudges permeated everything, including his manuscript pages . . .

and every part of Mitchell himself—shirt fronts, fingers, moustache, and hair."

There was no denying it, this wonderful storyteller, whose most famous work was *Who Has Seen The Wind* (often referred to as Who Has Seen the Waltons by Mitchell himself), inspired and entertained everyone around him when he lived here.

My last memory of him was from Calgary. He was bedridden. Merna had asked me to stop by, and I did. I talked a mile a minute, but Mitchell said nothing. It was as if I wasn't even there.

But just before I left, I turned and said, "You know, Andre is now playing hockey in the Czech Republic," and with that, I saw a smile break across his face and his eyes brighten.

I swear I could hear him silently cheering. [Nov. 17, 2005]

Now, Let's Talk About Me

Class Picture

I'M THE GUY IN THE BACK ROW, second from the left, the one with glasses slightly askew, and the long neck. "You look like such a geek!" my youngest son, Gabe, told me when I showed him last week.

I did. Pictures don't lie. I looked like I just got out of bed. My shirt was wrinkled and tight.

I remember that day in December 1962. My family had moved from Windsor to Bracebridge just a few years before. And here it was, now a week or so before Christmas. The photographer was supposed to have been there in October, but had come down with the flu, throwing off his entire schedule.

So now he was at the school. For some reason, he was in a terrible mood. Shuffling us about, shoving us into position, the whole time muttering about what a bunch of "useless twits" we all were. We didn't care. We laughed about it. At least until we thought this cameraman might slap my buddy Frankie.

"Hey fatty!" he shouted at my roly-poly pal. "Will you straighten up and look right at this!" pointing to the camera.

My own inattention was soon the cause of yet another explosion on the part of this mean-spirited curmudgeon.

"Hey four-eyes! Yes, you, ugly! You with those stupid glasses!"

Now he had my attention.

"Me?"

"Yes, you. Will you pay attention and not look like you're living on some other planet?"

I shrugged, and with the index finger of my right hand shifted my glasses higher up on my nose.

"Look straight ahead, buddy, willya!" he muttered.

I obeyed. I could feel my glasses however sliding back down my nose.

I shouted back, "Does this bother you?"

He looked up and after a moment said, "Bother me? What are you talking about?"

"My glasses." I responded.

"What about your glasses?" he asked, shaking his head like I had lost my marbles.

"My glasses . . . Do they bother you?"

He didn't respond. He turned away to load the camera.

"I asked you, do my glasses bother you? You said they were ugly. Or do you mean I am ugly? Which is it? And do my glasses bother you because they shift down on my nose?

"Or is it because they're crooked? Or is it the colour?"

It seemed I was talking a hundred miles an hour. At which point, the photographer cut me off. He'd had enough and bellowed: "I don't care about your stupid glasses! And yes, they are ugly, and yes, you're ugly, and all your friends here are ugly!

"Every last one of you!"

We were stunned. We stood in absolute silence—three stock-still rows of Grade 10 students. The girls in the front, some with plaid skirts, some with cap sleeve cotton dresses. The boys sporting flannel shirts or wool sweaters.

All of us shocked.

It had already been a horrible year for me. I had been streamed into the technical side, and forced to take "shop," where my days were spent toiling over lathes and making plumb bobs. I still don't know what a plumb bob is, and don't wish to find out.

But there I was along with my classmates, paralyzed and mute, when suddenly, in a squeaky tiny voice, Frankie started: "I wish you a Merry Christmas . . . I wish you a Merry Christmas . . ."

One by one our voices rose in unison until our song thundered and resonated throughout the gymnasium.

We were singing our hearts out.

The photographer just stood there. He didn't know what to say. I glanced at Frankie—immediately to my left—and he was beaming, his voice almost cracking.

I'd like to say the photographer clasped his hands over his ears. Or that he packed up his cameras and tripod and stormed out, and looked behind him in disgust. Or better still, that I could see him wiping away a tear before joining us in song.

None of that happened. He glared at us in total silence.

I smiled and once again, out of habit, shifted my glasses higher up on my nose, and mouthed something that in no way could be mistaken for "Merry Christmas." [Dec. 23, 2005]

I'VE BEEN AWAY. SICK. A common cold transformed quickly into pneumonia. I fought it every inch of the way, but last week when I hobbled into the clinic, the doctor took one glance at me and made the diagnosis. The whites of my eyes were red and leaking. My head was ready to burst. My lungs were clogged. I couldn't stop coughing. I was bundled up in the examining room with a scarf and mittens and toque. I looked like a consumptive figure out of a Charles Dickens novel.

This was after nearly a week of fighting what my wife had declared "the common cold." She'd sworn up and down that there was nothing to be done for it.

"Get out of bed! It's viral!"

For the first part of the week, I heeded her advice. I dutifully popped Echinacea like jellybeans. Then someone else informed me that I was using the wrong kind of Echinacea. The "Goldenseal" variety was what I needed. So, I switched to this, but my wife warned that if I had an allergy to goldenrod, this might not be a good idea.

Well, I'm in my 50s. I don't even know what goldenrod looks like. And so, bleary-eyed and sniffling, I flipped open Roger Tory Peterson's field guide and found it.

"Nope! Nothing like I've ever seen!"

More Golden Seal.

More Vitamin C.

More advice followed. I started gargling with Benzydamine for my acute sore throat and shooting Life Brand decongestant nasal spray up my nose. And to help me sleep—someone swore this would do the trick—I consumed the recommended dose of Tylenol Nighttime Sinus Relief. I also raided the medicine cabinet, and finished off an old bottle of Benylin First Defense "herbal cough syrup that boasted of combining Echinacea and menthol."

"That can't hurt," I concluded.

The cold worsened. I was up most of the night coughing. My wife fled to the spare bedroom. By then, I had stopped listening to her anyway. After all, she was the same person who dispatched me to a psychologist years ago when I was troubled with stomach problems.

"It's all in your head!" this man with a doctorate told me. He then hypnotized me and invited me to go on a journey of my intestinal tract with a repair kit to fix whatever ailed me.

I said, "This is not going to work—I hire people to fix my leaky faucets!"

My wife then dispatched me to a Windsor physician who subscribed to holistic medicine. He walked into the examining room, plunked himself down on a stool and brandishing a King James Bible confronted me: "Have you read this?"

I stammered: "Does it say something about people with intestinal problems?"

Things unravelled from there.

Finally, my own doctor sent me to a gastroenterologist. In 10 minutes he diagnosed me with Crohn's. Six months later, I was in surgery.

It baffles me as to why I take advice from people who have no medical background. A friend told me the other day that his wife snatched away all his high blood pressure medicine because she'd found a herbal cure for it.

"Where?" he asked.

"A woman at the supermarket," she told him.

Back to my "common cold." So, I'm in the clinic and being told I have developed pneumonia and need antibiotics. With that, I added Zithromax tablets to fight the infection as well as Moxifloxacin eye drops to counter the bacteria in my eyes.

Besides crunching and sucking on bag after bag of Ricola original Swiss Herb cough drops, I had also sought the support of Imovane, a sleep medication.

My wife—miffed and skeptical—returned home with a small bottle of Calmylin (with codeine) to fight my aggravating cough.

"It's all you need—it fights cough, nasal and chest congestion . . ."

She spooned two teaspoons of this into my mouth, and within minutes, I had entered the realm of Timothy Leary. I lay paralyzed on the couch. Stoned. I could hear my voice carrying on a lively conversation with my thighs and ordering them to move on command.

I prayed for angels to bear me away. [Feb. 15, 2005]

The Pen

I'M WRITING THIS COLUMN WITH A FOUNTAIN PEN. A green marble hand-finished pen made by Visconti in Florence, Italy. It's called Pericles, a pen that is normally manufactured in pearlized colours with a hinge clip that resembles Pericles's own headgear.

The ink flows freely in broad strokes as I move the nib across the page.

Smooth, graceful, refined.

A lost art, really.

It occurred to me that few of us pay any attention at all to fountain pens.

It's difficult even finding one in a world that has embraced the roller ball or the ballpoint. But when I was in elementary school in Riverside, I sat at a wooden desk and wrote with a cheap fountain pen bought at the dime store.

Every September, our mothers would buy us a new pen and a bottle of Waterman ink. And we'd dip our nibs into the ink bottles cradled in those inkwells at the corner of our desks. From about Grade 3 onward, we learned penmanship. They call it "cursive writing" today. Back when I was in school, I'm not sure what they called it, but we used a floppy exercise notebook and busied ourselves with all those curls and swirls and loops and zigzags. It might've been the Palmer Method. In any case, we were engaged in formal lessons every morning, slumped over our desks, sculpting out those letters from the alphabet, and filling page after page with inverse tornado-like figures.

After a while, we were writing out little hearts out, writing over and over again the sentence, "The Quick Brown Fox jumps Over the Lazy Dog." We wrote it until our hands were sore. We wrote in fear the nun patrolling the aisles would suddenly rap us across the knuckles if we didn't get it right, or if for one lazy lapse, we slowed down.

We all experienced this. It was part of our upbringing in Ontario. We grew up in the same kind of classroom. Writing with cheap fountain pens that sometimes could be turned into "weapons,' says Brantford poet John B. Lee.

"We would siphon up the ink and flick it at the fellow across the aisle, or we'd poke the girl in front of us with our pen."

Lee says the exercise of learning longhand failed him: "I now half-write and half-print . . . I have about seven different styles. If you look at my notebooks, it looks like seven different people wrote in them."

I suffered the same fate. One might call it "cursed writing."

Not everyone, of course, shares this.

A former Windsor elementary school teacher once told me she was so good at it in Grade 3, her teacher led her down the hall to the Grade 8 class to show them how "flawless" her writing was. The teacher told her students, "If she can do this in Grade 3, you can certainly do it in Grade 8!"

Today, the computer dominates. Keyboarding is the way. Cursive writing is irrelevant, what with the world of debit, and internet banking, making it practically unnecessary to even know how to sign your name.

In a piece by Robert Kose in the Christian Science-Monitor, he recounts what it was like in the 1950s: "When I asked (my latter-day grammar teacher) if she valued good handwriting in her students, she looked puzzled, as if I had addressed her in Albanian . . ."

As for the fountain pen? Dead in schools. The keyboard is faster. Easier to read. But there are still those who use them. Once, when I went into a doctor's office and was just beginning to spill out my tales of medical woes, this specialist leaned over and plucked my pen from my shirt pocket.

"This is nice! A Parker Duofold!" he said admiring it. The next few minutes, that's all we talked about.

It's been a while since I've used such glorious writing instruments. This new fountain pen, bought over the internet, has reawakened the aesthetics of writing. I realize now it means slowing down, like stopping outside your door and taking a deep breath. It means giving thought to what you write.

I'm amazed at its smoothness and richness on the page. It's then I remembered a Paris shopkeeper telling me years ago when I bought a Waterman from him: "The pen's liquid is like wine—it goes down effortlessly . . ."

True enough.

But now I must transfer this turquoise ink into type. [Feb. 10, 2004]

One Square Inch Of The Yukon

SOMEWHERE IN THE MOVE TO WINDSOR IN THE LATE 1960s, I lost the deed to a property up north. I've searched and searched for this piece of paper, but to no avail. I think I tacked it to a wall in my bedroom, and when my parents departed the city, they might've left it attached to the wall.

Now I am sitting in a coffee shop with a friend, and the conversation comes around to the 1950s when the two of us acquired property in the Yukon. Of course, we never saw it—we were barely ten. We weren't even allowed out at night without our parents.

But like millions of other kids swept up in the idea of owning the land of Sergeant Preston, I dug my grimy hands into a box of Quaker Puffed Rice for this "Deed of Land" document from The Klondike Big Inch Land Company. I vividly recall staring at the vignette of a man panning for gold, and studying the signature of the company's president, John Baker, Jr. I pinned the deed to the upstairs bedroom wall on Prado Place in old Riverside. I can only guess it was 1955.

My father, however, set me straight about this piece of paper, saying this was all a hoax. For me, it was like learning Santa Claus didn't exist. The deeds turned out to be worthless, or almost.

Let me tell you the story behind that deed and The Klondike Big Inch's promotional campaign initiated by Quaker Oats Company in 1954. It stemmed from the popular radio show in 1953 called Sergeant Preston of the Yukon. It featured the adventures of this Royal Canadian Mounted Police officer and his dog, Yukon King. But while the show itself was popular, Quaker found difficulty hawking its Puffed Wheat and Puffed Rice cereals. Along came advertising executive Bruce Baker with the inspired notion of stuffing boxes of Puffed Wheat and Puffed Rice with land deeds. Quaker's legal experts said registering this deed for millions of kids would be a nightmare. Baker responded: "Well, don't!" He convinced the Canadian government to sell 19.11 acres of land that could be subdivided and given away without registering individual deeds.

Baker's proved to be perhaps one of the most popular advertising campaigns in history. The company couldn't keep up with the demand. But really, did these one inch Yukon lands exist? The late

George Van Roggen, a former senator, dealt with Baker when the Chicago-based advertising genius asked if the Canadian government would sell some property. The Yukon lawyer found Baker a parcel of land 11 km up the Yukon River from Dawson for a price tag of $1,000.

In an article in *Canadian Magazine*, Jack McIver describes how Van Roggen took Baker out in an open skiff to inspect his land. In drawing up the deeds, Quaker's legal minds were careful to state that purchase of these one inch properties excluded "mineral rights." It also stipulated that "perpetual access or easement across their land would be granted."

Van Roggen also provided a means of easily subdividing the land. The deeds—numbering 21 million—were arranged consecutively, according to a master plan. He told *Canadian Magazine*: "If you wanted to find lot number 11,935,000, you simply had to start at the northwest corner of the land, travel east 7,000 inches, go south 1,705 inches, and there you'd be, standing on your inch."

It was all a gimmick.

Some, however, took ownership seriously. One fellow travelled all over the U.S. collecting these deeds until he had 10,880. He calculated this would add up to 75 square feet. He then asked Quaker's legal department "to consolidate the different inches into one big chunk." He also preferred a piece of land "near the water" and "as quiet as possible."

In another instance, a man convicted of killing his wife with an ice pick, hired a defence attorney with the promise of signing over his property in the Yukon. The lawyer withdrew his support when he discovered the client's parcel of land consisted of 1,000 Quaker Oats deeds.

Whatever happened to this property?

Well, the Klondike Big Inch Company failed to pay back taxes of $37.20, and as a result, in January 1965, ownership reverted to the Canadian government. However, word is these deeds will fetch as much as $90 from collectors of memorabilia.

Go figure. [May 4, 2005]

THIS MIGHT SOUND CRAZY. Before today, I would never have thought how the death of a refrigerator might be like the passing of a great aunt, or a grandfather. Someone who has always been a part of your life. Like the 18.4 cubic-foot white Kenmore in our home. It is older than my 14-year-old son. He's never known any other fridge. Never contemplated its inevitable demise. For him, it's a non-issue. It's always been there. Always that doleful hum of the motor. Always ready to please. Now it's sick. On its last legs, and ready to shudder one last time before it finally croaks.

My son—and for that matter, my wife—refuse to talk about it. They're in denial. They can't believe it.

Or won't.

I understand.

From the surface, it seems little has changed.

The face of the fridge still beams with a youthful glow, enhanced no doubt by the cheery-looking magnets that pin a succession of miniature photos of our three sons in hockey uniforms spanning some 20 years, an outdated workout schedule for a daughter who left home eight years ago, an assortment of baby pictures, a grocery list and a sticky note announcing we're out of toilet paper.

The fridge remains the repository of a disorganized life. Always there—unfailing, faithful, sure and steady. And so dispensing with it isn't the same as pushing an old couch that has suffered the ravages of puppies and cigarette burns to the edge of the road in the hopes of it being scooped up. You drive by them, and feel nothing.

On the other hand, when you spot a fridge at the curb, a different emotion stirs in your breast. They are rarely seen. For good reason. The average life span of a fridge is 20 years, according to Lawrence Berkeley Laboratories. Most last 14 to 15 years before finally giving up the ghost.

The writer Nick Cave says "the fridge delays death; it fights against death, fights against nature. This cuboid of cool is a rebel against time . . ." And while the fridge is that instrument that defies death, it can't stop itself from expiring.

But it tries. And it tugs away at us, the memories of waking in the summer and padding across the floor and opening the door—a pool of light flooding the kitchen—and reaching inside for a cold piece of apple pie.

Or what about the fridge in the garage? The beer repository. Its sole purpose to keep the beer cold.

This week such thoughts as these swarmed my brain as I watched my wife tend to the fridge, mopping up the pool of water that had formed on the floor beneath it.

"Oh, it's nothing!" she said.

Denial.

And so, feeling much like a selfish and cold-hearted son-in-law eager to dump the old bat in a nursing home, I began to make the rounds to the appliance stores.

The sales people actually expressed concern: "What's wrong with the old one?"

"It's leaking!"

"Oh, that's too bad," they all said with what appeared to be genuine concern. Most offered to pick up the old fridge, assuring me that its parts could be recycled. Like the harvesting of organs of the body? A heart, a lung, a kidney? It made me wonder if fridges ought to come with donor cards. It warmed my heart that maybe whatever life might still beat within, it could live again in the shell of another.

Maybe.

Meanwhile, at home, my wife was busy sprucing up the old Kenmore, washing down the shelves, desperately trying to make the old lady look youthful and healthy.

But someone has to do the dirty work . . . and pull the plug. [Oct. 12, 2004]

The Typewriter

SOMEWHERE TUCKED AWAY IN MY HOUSE are two portable typewriters. They sit in cases. Unused. Abandoned. Nearly forgotten. Frozen in time.

My youngest son—15 years old—rooting around for something else, stumbled across one of these machines, and pulled it out of its case. "Hey Dad, what is this?" Before I could answer, Gabe was firing more questions at me. "Where's the cord? I mean, where do you plug this in? And where's the monitor?"

It never occurred to me he wouldn't know anything about a typewriter. By that, I mean he knew it was a typewriter, but its function, or how it worked, initially was a mystery. As he examined this contraption, my son naively asked all these questions, only to wind up concluding that this old Royal didn't function like a computer.

No screen. No electrical plug.

However, it did have a tiny bell that sounded each time you neared the far right side of the page. At which point, you had to slide the carriage lever over and push the typewriter's carriage all the way to the right. It would automatically skip down to the next line and bring you back to the left edge of the page.

Of course, what I've just written would probably baffle and confound a person who has never used a typewriter.

Lever? Carriage? Page?

Mind you, my bespectacled typewriting teacher from high school whose world was one of ribbon spools, space bars, carriage release levers, platen knobs and typebars, would be equally confused if I drilled him with terms like pixels, word processing software, downloads, RAM, and jpegs.

In a sentimental way, I remember being dispatched to the typewriting class.

We didn't call it keyboarding. It wasn't word processing. It was typing. I was the only boy in Grade 10 who took the course, having been exiled from "shop," the room in the basement crowded with lathes and where we fashioned plumb bobs. My incompetence got the better of me and I was asked to join "the girls" in typing. The typewriters there were equipped with keyboards bereft of letters, numbers and symbols. We learned "touch typing." As it turned out, this was probably the only class I took in high school that prepared me for what I do today.

Algebra? Geometry? Chemistry? The only thing I remember of them are the doodles I scribbled in my textbooks.

But those big stand-up Underwoods held a fascination for me, and still do.

"Typewriters have been consigned to the dustbin of history, but their ghosts are everywhere," says Darren Wershler-Henry in his book *The Iron Whim: A Fragmented History of Typewriting*. I can agree with this. It's true. Somehow we are drawn sentimentally, perhaps, or aesthetically, to the "look" of the old typewriter, or as the author says, to those "pixel-perfect damaged letters that sit crookedly above or below the line with paradoxical consistency . . ."

Across the street from me at the Windsor Community Museum, there are letters penned from the late Morley Callaghan (friend of Hemingway and Stein) to Raymond Knister. These letters, drafted in the 1920s, are typewritten, and in a curious way the page displays the eccentricities of Callaghan himself, or more specifically, his typewriter.

In a curious way, each typewriter has its own fingerprint. Some writers might never find the time to correct the way the letter "h" might strike the page, and so it might remain a little faint, or it might jump slightly above other letters in what otherwise would have been a straight line of type. As a result, it's somewhat easier for scholars to trace the identity of an unsigned letter back to the author, simply by the caprices of the typewriter used.

This speaks volumes about the "character" of the typewriter and its personality. And maybe the personalities who used them.

In this newsroom in the 1950s, a certain columnist, so incensed over his typewriter jamming up and slowing him at deadline, heaved it out the second-floor window onto Ferry Street.

What's missing from this newsroom is the echo of the clacking typewriter from every corner, the black smudge left on the thumb and index finger from the filthy carbon paper we slipped between the sheets of newsprint we typed on. [Mar. 10, 2006]

Father's Day

WITH FATHER'S DAY APPROACHING SUNDAY, I got to thinking maybe there ought to be report cards on dads whose sons and daughters play competitive sport.

I know many such dads. And you can't help but ask: How do I measure up? Did I pass with flying colours? Do I need re-training?

I spend enough time with such creatures. I idle with them behind the glass along the ice surface of arenas. I sit with them in other arenas during the summer, witnessing our sons murder each other on the floor with lacrosse sticks. We learn a lot about each other.

We can't help but measure ourselves against one another. I know they laugh at me during the annual father-son games. They laugh even harder when they learn I haven't got my head around the meaning of the "interference" penalty in hockey.

I always argue, "That's got to be good thing, right? I mean, that's what hockey is. Interference, right?"

But back to the report card. I know what you're thinking. Sure, there are dads who 'lose it' in the stands—mothers too. I've seen them embarrass themselves and their kids by shouting and picking fights, and in some cases, even running off between cars in the parking lot to duke it out.

I've heard dads bad-mouthing each other and the other sons on the team. I'm sure I've done it too. We all do.

I've seen dads do the unthinkable. One fellow left his son behind at a Woodstock arena because he was so embarrassed by his play. He drove home, forcing his boy to arrange a ride with another father.

I can't excuse such behaviour. And won't. But let me say this. I've seen dads take time off from work—and lose pay—to make sure their son or daughter got to the rink on time. Why? Because they wouldn't miss it for the world.

I've seen dads hurry their hurt sons to the hospital, holding back tears because there was nothing else they could do but navigate the car. I've seen them console their boys over a coach's angry words. I've seen them rise at dawn and dress their six-year-old tykes in full uniform, carry them to their snow-covered cars and drive them to frigid arenas.

I've seen them suffer with their kids when other kids are mean to theirs and tell them they don't belong on the team. I've seen them regularly drop loonies into the arena dispensing machines to make sure there's Gatorade for after the game.

I've seen these dads stand outside, waiting and waiting, slapping each player on the back and telling them they've had a good game, even if they hadn't. It's what we do. It's about meaning well. It's about encouragement. It's all about keeping the focus on the positives, even though we privately despair over the loss of a game, or how our own son screwed up.

But we keep that to ourselves. We do that. We do it as easily as breathing.

And sure there are moments of frustration. Like when we drop off our kids at the arena, head off to Tim's for a coffee and are just getting settled into our seats when we spot our son making his way from the dressing room—all dressed in his equipment minus his skates.

"Dad, can you go home and get my skates—I left them in the garage."

We might want to curse. Sometimes maybe we do. But the other dads and moms are there, and we spot them smirking.

And we know why.

It's happened to them. Their kids have forgotten mouth guards. Their boys have forgotten athletic supports. Their sons have forgotten team jerseys.

Yes, we run home and fetch whatever has been mislaid. And we fume over this, and swear it'll never happen again. But we know we will do it all over again. We do this because we know there's no choice.

Call it duty. Call it crazy. Call it love.

That's why we are put on earth. [June 14, 2006]

THE LAST DAY OF SUMMER. The first day of school. It was never easy making the transition.

Yet it was pretty simple when I was growing up. There seemed to be little philosophical interference on the part of educators. We were expected to do the basic things: reading, writing, and arithmetic.

Sink or swim.

You either passed or failed. You either got it or you didn't.

If you didn't succeed, the education system never resorted to defining it by some florid name like ADD (attention deficit disorder). No one talked about Ritalin. They simply branded you as "slow."

I fell under that classification every year. I was a daydreamer. I stared endlessly out the window. Or I endlessly counted the perforations in the classroom's ceiling tiles. Or peeled away gum wads under my desk. Or meticulously timed the pauses the principal made in the morning announcements.

For punishment, I cleaned brushes on the school steps. I also wrote out what seemed to be a thousand lines on the blackboard: "I don't pay attention in school . . . I don't pay attention in school . . ."

It was difficult seeing summer come to an end, only to begin *that* again.

Each year, our parents would build a bonfire in the schoolyard the night before school opened, and they'd cart out coolers of beer and watch us cavort in the eerie darkness. We'd run about with straightened out coat hangers that had been sharpened at one end in some neighbourhood machine shop. We'd use these to roast hot dogs or marshmallows.

There'd always be a ballgame on the radio, or Pat Boone's mellifluous voice spilling out in the darkness.

Life was sweet in the summers of the late 1950s. School on the other hand was always tough that first day, that first week. Like others, I was always anxious to make a good impression, and fell under the innocent belief that just maybe they'd forget what I was like the year before. They never did.

In my last year at a Catholic school in Windsor—Grade 6—I figured I could change my reputation. We had to write that tired old assignment, How I Spent My Summer Holidays. So I began my story in a way that I figured would win approval. I expected it would melt the hearts of the Sisters of St. Joseph. I began the story this way:

Every morning during the summer, I went to Our Lady of Guadalupe Church to serve mass. Every morning, I helped out in cleaning the church. I also stayed after mass to study Latin . . . I did this because I want to become a priest and dedicate my life to Holy Mother Church.

With that, I was immediately summoned to the office of the principal, Sister Mary of Perpetual Help. Her smile was as broad as the horizon, and her eyes danced with delight at the revelation that I wanted to be a priest.

"A priest!" she squealed with pleasure.

"Yes," I said.

"Well, I am so proud of you. And so surprised! Not everybody is cut out to be a priest."

"I know that," I said, trying to sound mature and wise at eleven.

"Well . . ." she paused, "I think we can help you! And maybe, we should have done so all along."

It had worked. I was a special case. All because I told them I wanted to be a priest. I danced all the way home, privately cheering my ingenious ruse. What I could not foresee was what unfolded the next day: an unexpected visit from the parish priest.

I spotted him in the hallway outside my class, chatting with Sister Mary of Perpetual Help. My face turned red, and she noticed. I started to sweat. You see, I hadn't gone to church all summer. I hadn't swept the floors in the sanctuary. I hadn't studied Latin after mass. I hadn't done any of these things. I'd lied. And that was a sin.

When I looked up, I could see that Sister Mary was annoyed and glaring at me in a way that suggested it was now certain I was going straight to hell. [Aug. 30, 2002]

Paris Hospital

MOST PEOPLE WHO GET ON A PLANE AND TRAVEL TO PARIS return home with pictures of the Eiffel Tower, the Louvre and Notre Dame.

I jetted home with X-rays of my bowel, the architecture of my insides. Late last month, my wife and I arrived at Charles de Gaulle Airport on the early morning flight from Toronto, and made our way down to our favourite hotel on Boulevard Port Royal. A place no more than a 15-minute stroll to the Closerie des Lilas, the café where Hemingway worked on his short stories and met with Scott Fitzgerald and Ezra Pound.

It's a hotel that has been operated by the same family for more than 70 years and where in the early 1900s the state executioner used to spend the night before walking down the street at 5:00 A.M. just a few short blocks to the prison to carry out his grim duties. It's also only a few minutes away from Rue St. Jacques where Hopital Cochin Saint-Vincent-De-Paul is located.

Alas, it was here—in this hospital—that I spent my first night in the city.

Decked out in the universal blue johnny-shirt, and hooked up to an IV, struggling to beat back the pain in my gut from yet another flare-up with Crohn's, a debilitating bowel disease.

It gave me some cause for reflection while I was lying there.

The triage nurse was surprisingly unfazed by the fact I handled French about as well as a toddler just learning the language. I found myself reduced to sentences with only nouns and speaking loudly as if this would substitute for verbs. This nurse put me at ease when she gently placed the index finger of her right hand on my lips to tell me to stop.

"Monsieur, maladie de Crohn!" she said matter-of-factly.

I was relieved she understood, much like when you're frantically fumbling through a phrase book in a Paris cafe and the waiter casually supplies the word for the dessert you're inquiring about.

"Crème Brûlée, monsieur?"

So there I was in emergency—on the advice of the hotel concierge—and surveying a place swarming with sick people. So many, in fact, they were leaning, slumped against the walls. One woman with a

193

mashed nose. A teenager doubled over in pain. A kid with a fever rocked by a gentle father. And more.

"It'll be a long time," I despaired.

To my surprise, within 15 minutes I was led to a room where three nurses awaited my arrival.

As sexist as this might sound—and I apologize for that—under the circumstances, this was one moment of bliss in all that pain, having these three young attractive French nurses with pouty lips taking blood, fitting an IV, and doing an EKG. And when that was completed, I was shifted down the hall to radiology for X-rays.

In the course of the first 20 minutes, I had seen two doctors, and now waited for word from the gastroenterologist and a surgeon.

Back home, my own doctor told me this would have taken 10 to 12 hours.

The doctor running me through all these tests was a fascinating character. It wasn't long before we shifted the medical concerns to the economy of language in Hemingway's work, talked about Gertrude Stein. He told me a story about crazy Zelda Fitzgerald, Scott's wife, who in the 1920s had ordered a mechanic to sever the top of their new Renault when they were in the south of France. The couple got caught in a major downpour, abandoned the automobile, and hopped a train to Paris.

Fitzgerald then petitioned Hemingway to help him retrieve the car. On that trip south, Fitzgerald fell ill, and Hemingway—placating his new friend's questionable illness—wound up employing a room thermometer to take his temperature.

But my Parisian doctor—Yann Erick Claessens—also raved about the sauces and wine, and tasting the escargot at Closerie des Lilas. But I was in not in a state to dine.

I waited for the surgeon. I half expected a fiftyish man with a Gauloises-stained handlebar mustache and broad hands. Instead, when I glanced up, I saw this gorgeous angel—a sweet apparition with a stethoscope gliding through the door.

The surgeon?

"Monsieur, I am the surgeon," she said. "Do you mind if I feel all over your stomach?"

Take your time. Take your time. [Mar. 10, 2005]

WHEN I STEPPED BACK STAGE AT THE FOX THEATRE, and spotted one of the Rockettes slowly and silently rehearsing a few dance steps on the dark floors, and noticed another dancer going through some stretching exercises, I realized I didn't belong there.

In the dim recesses of this sanctuary, the real entertainers were preparing for the show they'd been doing nightly. Moments later, more Rockettes began to appear. Slim glittering outfits, long legs that stretched all the way to heaven, faces as bright as stars in the night sky.

I guess I expected entertainers with sore feet, bad nerves, or a banal tune night after night faltering and bouncing in their brains. But my thoughts were lost in this bewildering array of back stage glamour. Yet I still had the presence of mind to notice a plate of cookies on a table in a nearby cubbyhole. I also saw stagehands moving what looked like a set into place. I could hear a restless audience beyond the curtains in seats where I normally would be sitting.

But this was my night. My debut at the Fox. My glory in the lights. My 15-minutes of fame. Showbiz. The warm up act for the world famous Radio City Rockettes, described as "the beloved icon and true slice of Americana."

I wasn't alone. I was accompanied by entertainment writer Ted Shaw and the much-younger advertising saleswoman Tina Lavigne, who easily could be mistaken for a Rockette, except for her outfit.

We were there to read Clement C. Moore's classic 19th-century poem "The Night Before Christmas."

We stood at centre stage behind the curtain, and our directions raced through our brains like algebraic equations reminding us to move forward on cue. We were to move, and find our way to our seats on decorative boxes.

A couple of nights earlier, others conscripted to read from Moore's book failed dismally in getting the audience to cheer on Dasher and Dancer, and Prancer and Vixen, Comet and Cupid, and Donner and Blitzen.

We had something else in mind.

We were going to ad lib the story, pretend we were hardboiled editors, and seriously interrupt Tina's reading of the story at every turn.

Her role was to be the intern who wanted us to publish a new story she'd written about Christmas.

In essence, we intended to expunge every silly archaism from the work, update it, and make it 21st-century material. It was supposed to be comical. It was at this point, just before I stepped out on stage that I began to panic: What if they don't laugh? What if they don't get it?

It was too late.

Our names were being announced, and the curtain was opening. I felt paralyzed. I could feel my heart pounding against the bones in my chest. And when I glanced behind me, I swear one of the Rockettes winked at me, and this nearly made me tumble through the curtains and out on the stage. It reminded me of being six at the 1952 Christmas school concert when I misunderstood the nun's instructions for us to wear a suit. We were supposed to be reindeer. So I pestered my mom to buy me a reindeer suit. She refused. Instead, she decked me out in a bear outfit and fitted cardboard antlers to my head. So there I was, the only kid in Grade 2 filing out on stage with my friends wearing this silly costume. The others all wore suits and ties. The audience broke into laughter.

More bad memories seeped out in that last moment. I thought, "Wouldn't my mother be proud?" Then realized she'd never cough up the dough for this ticket, even if *I* were a Rockette.

But you can't think of such things on stage, not in the midst of a performance. Now we were into it. And the audience was beginning to laugh at our jokes. We were building momentum. Tina read well, and Ted and I were perfect curmudgeons. Now we were feeling the magic, and I began to think maybe my cellphone might start ringing with requests to do this again. Then suddenly the lights over us began to dim. But our mouths were still moving—we weren't finished. Hey, what gives? We had another couple of lines.

That's when I saw the stage manager waiting for us at the bottom of the stage with our coats.

We were being given the hook. [Dec. 23, 2005]

The Art Of Snow Shovelling

I HAVE DISCOVERED ONLY NOW, after 35 years of marriage, that the true test of matrimonial bliss is shovelling out the driveway.

Together. As a couple.

I was raised to believe this a man's job. Five decades of Canadian Tire propaganda provided strong reinforcement, with ads showing strong men examining proper shovels and doing what men do with them, shovelling out driveways and walkways for women and children.

Somehow over the years, I had forgotten why I ever left this role to my wife. I had begun to believe it was because she wanted exercise. Yearned to fill her lungs with the crisp winter air. Yearned never to let winter pass without tasting the enervating experience of dealing with the snowy elements. I thought she liked shovelling snow.

And so when the first real snowfall of the year hit the area— 19CM—I decided to break with tradition and venture out to clean off the driveway. By 6:30 P.M., I had gone over it twice. Feeling ambitious, I also did the walk and the porch. I even went next door and cleared the path to my neighbour's door. I was quite proud of myself, because, as I say, I usually leave this for my wife.

But the snow kept falling. At 9:00 P.M. I was back out. My wife said she would join me, but needed to change. Meaning, of course, her clothes, not her attitude.

But why change? I don't know. It's not as if she had just been out in a cocktail dress. The fact is, men don't have to change. They don't dress for the occasion. They wear whatever they've got on.

In 10 minutes—that's how long it took my wife to find the appropriate clothes for shovelling out the driveway—I had already completed most of the job.

Or so I thought.

My wife appeared. She shook her head in disapproval, then started going over what I had just done. I imagined this is what boot camp must be like—the scowling sergeant with a riding crop messing up blankets on the already-made bed because he spotted one ripple.

Anyway, there was my wife scraping right down to the concrete. There she was carefully sculpting the walled banks of snow along the edges of the driveway, reminding me how meticulous her own father had been. On this very driveway. (Another thing, I have learned: Never move into your wife's childhood home. Paying the mortgage doesn't make it yours. It's always hers. Until her death does she depart.)

I gleefully told her we could start this together. Wouldn't that be nice? Husband and wife toiling together, side by side. A union of loving souls.

I made the mistake of telling her I had borrowed a neighbour's shovel.

"Oh, let me use it!" she said.

"Why?" I countered.

"Because you see our shovel—the edges of it are curled from someone not using it properly. So let me have her (the neighbour's) shovel."

"But why? Do you think I did that damage to our shovel?"

"Well," she shrugged, "someone did. And it wasn't me."

That, of course, left only one other person. Still, I wouldn't give her the shovel. That would be an admission of guilt. I left the driveway to her and started on the sidewalk. I even used it to clear the snow off my car on the road. I could see from her silence that she didn't approve.

So I shouted across the yard, "Maybe you could teach snow shovelling at St. Clair College. A night course!"

No response. She was busy.

"Ever thought of driving a Zamboni?"

No response.

"What about using a toothbrush!"

No response.

My wife was busy, having divided the driveway into quadrants, to work each one of them horizontally, pushing the snow to the banks, then sculpting each bank like a hockey rink's boards.

My approach had been different. Speeding like a maniac down the driveway with the shovel, pushing the snow helter-skelter. Hers was deliberate and methodical, each swipe a part of an overall plan. One quadrant at a time.

Forty minutes later, she was done.

The Art Of Snow Shovelling

Long after everyone was in bed, about 12:30 A.M., I slipped on my boots and quietly went outside. I stood in the silence of the driveway. Then changed my mind about burying her car in the very snow she had shovelled out. [Jan. 16, 2004]

I DREAD THIS TIME OF THE YEAR. This is when I lose control.

As the days tick down to Christmas, my wife spends her evenings wrapping presents, playing Christmas CDs, baking cookies—and transforming the entire house into what I call "Christmas Land."

This is usually the week my wife runs out to pluck a tree from a street vendor, haggles with him and examines the tree as carefully as a breeder might examine the offspring of a famous race horse.

Long ago, she lost faith in my ability to buy a Christmas tree. One year, she returned a tree I had picked up and scolded the vendor for selling me this skeletal pine, and told him I was an idiot for driving away with it.

A year ago, my wife, fuming over her own choice of a Christmas tree that was obviously not "fresh," because it rained needles to the floor every time you shut a door, stripped all the decorations off and drove it back to the lot.

She came home with a new one.

Actually, it's not uncommon for her to do this.

Meanwhile, our family retreats in embarrassment.

When it comes to decorating the tree, we long ago gave up trying.

Initially we're eager to help, even encouraged to do so. But as soon as we reach out to place a twinkling Christmas bauble on the tree, we get our wrists slapped.

"No, no, silly! Not there!"

Almost as if we'd tried to hang a dirty sock on the tree.

We eventually retreat to some other part of the house, like a dog that has just soiled the carpet and can't figure out what it's done. And so my wife completes the job of the tree.

Then out comes the other stuff.

We have many nativity sets, culled from trips to Germany, Israel, Portugal, England and Poland. One by one, they slip out of carefully packed boxes and make their way to the mantel above the fireplace. Soon, the arrangement of these mangers side by side begins to remind me of a subdivision. This could be Forest Glade. But my youngest son corrects me and pipes up, "It looks more like a ghetto!"

True enough.

Usually about this time, our advent calendar with the chocolates hidden by each little cardboard door makes its appearance.

We're usually late with this. It means gobbling up the chocolates right up to the 12th or 13th. One year, Gabe, my youngest, ate them all before we made it to the second week. Maybe that's why my wife doesn't set up the calendar until the third week of December.

But the room isn't done. Not yet.

There are the wreaths. One positioned over the fireplace, another over the side door, and one on the outside door.

And what about the Christmas lights on the porch railings? In past years, I've seen my wife outside on Christmas morning toiling at getting the lights to work.

But inside the house is a different matter. She's organized. She's meticulous. She's overwhelming. Out come the armies of Christmas figurines: miniature angels playing musical instruments, tiny wooden Bavarian houses from some faraway Christmas village, wise men bearing gifts of frankincense and myrrh, illuminated Santa Clauses, including one on a motorcycle, shepherds, baby Jesuses, Mary look-a-likes, two or three Josephs, illuminated artificial tabletop angel Christmas trees, Santa's little helpers and various sleighs and one figure I'd swear looks like Darth Vader.

At this point, I'm defeated. I wearily climb the stairs to a little office I keep as a place of refuge. My space. Once there, I settle back into a comfy chair, and read something that will help me sleep, maybe send me into a temporary coma that will end in January, when everything is packed away. Late in January, just to be on the safe side.

I choose Edward Gibbon's 1,360-page *Decline and Fall of the Roman Empire.* The bookmark indicates last Christmas I didn't get past page 29.

I've got the rest of my life. [Dec. 12, 2005]

201

Index

About The Author

MARTY GERVAIS IS. THE AUTHOR OF MORE THAN 20 BOOKS of poetry, fiction, non-fiction and drama. In 1998 he won the prestigious Harbourfront Festival Prize for his contribution to Canadian literature. In 1997, he won the Milton Acorn People's Poetry Award for his collection *Tearing Into A Summer Day*.

Gervais' most successful book *The Rumrunners*, was a bestseller in 1980, and has sold more than 25,000 copies since. A new, revised edition, published by Biblioasis, will appear in the fall of 2008.

Gervais has worked for a number of newspapers. For 17 years, he was *The Windsor Star*'s book editor. Currently he writes the thrice-weekly "My Town" column, from which this book derives. He has won more than a dozen newspaper awards for his work.

He is also the University of Winsdor's "resident writing professional," where he offers creative writing workshops to the public.

In addition to his own writing, Marty Gervais is the publisher of Black Moss Press, one of Canada's oldest independent publishing houses.